Some of the steps described in this activist's handbook are obvious. You can refrain from buying fur coats, refuse to hunt for recreation, and offer your home to a homeless animal.

But these steps are not enough. Virtually every aspect of your lifestyle, consuming habits, and community consciousness can be geared toward animal protection, as well . . .

The animal activist must also be an environmentalist. After all, saving the biosphere—the living earth—means fighting global warming; saving the oceans; and protecting the rain forests . . .

What's more, as today's environmentalists point out, the future of the earth's animals will ultimately be our own. If our consuming habits remain the same, and if, as predicted, our population doubles, we will leave precious few resources for ourselves—let alone for the other species of the earth.

We believe that if each human being would follow the steps in this simple handbook, the animals of the earth would truly be saved, and our own future and quality of life secured.

—from the Introduction

· YOU CAN ·
SAVE THE
ANIMALS
—50—
THINGS TO DO
Right Now

Dr. Michael W. Fox &
Pamela Weintraub

ST. MARTIN'S PAPERBACKS

YOU CAN SAVE THE ANIMALS: 50 THINGS TO DO RIGHT NOW

Copyright © 1991 by Dr. Michael W. Fox and Pamela Weintraub.

ISBN: 0-312-92521-2

Printed in the United States of America

St. Martin's Paperbacks edition/February 1991

10 9 8 7 6 5 4 3 2 1

Acknowledgments

The authors gratefully acknowledge the invaluable resource materials provided by various animal- and environmental-protection organizations. Particularly, we would like to thank the Humane Society of the United States. We also wish to thank our editor, Bob Weil, for his deep commitment to and support of this book, and Richard Romano, also of St. Martin's Press.

Contents

III
Food for Thought

IV
The Compassionate Consumer

V
The Discriminating Dresser

VI
Ferocious Frivolities

VII
Call of the Wild

VIII
The Community of Conscience

IX
The Political Animal

Introduction

Every day more than two hundred elephants are gunned down on the savannas and in the forests of Africa by ruthless bands of poachers armed with automatic rifles. These poachers, operating in violation of the law, are seeking white gold—the ivory tusks of elephants, which, because they are carved into jewelry, trinkets, and piano keys, bring up to $240 a pound on the open market. Millions of elephants once roamed the vast continent of Africa, but if the bloody massacre for ivory continues, the elephant will become extinct.

On the modern factory-style farm, animals face different problems. But their plight is just as grave. Chickens are stuffed into small wire cages arranged in tiers called battery cages, veal calves are cramped inside pens so small that they can't turn around, and livestock and poultry are variously fed hormones and chemical additives and stimulated to accelerated growth through the use of glaring lights kept on night and day. Yet other animals live in perpetual semidarkness to keep them docile under conditions that would normally engender unbearable aggression and stress.

Indeed, animals are routinely clubbed for their fur, shot with arrows for fun, subjected to painful experiments, and raised and slaughtered under inhumane conditions for their meat. The greenhouse effect—caused by man's overuse of fossil fuels and the destruction of the world's rain forests, among other things—threatens to raise the earth's temperature several degrees over the next hundred years, resulting in mass extinctions. The extra ultraviolet radiation reaching the earth due to depletion of the ozone layer threatens animals and their food sources. And the destruction of ecosystems from the rain forest to delicate marine habitats could result in the loss of more than half the animal and insect species in the world. According to some grim estimates, the world's species are becoming extinct at the rate of 150,000 per year, or 17 per hour.

In fact, common sense spells out the obvious: We cannot hope to save the environment and ignore the animal kingdom at the same time. The extinction of animal species intensifies environmental degradation and promotes ecological disease and dysfunction. Animal suffering under our dominion is a symptom of a destructively uncaring relationship to the earth. Saving our planet and its multitude of species does not mean placing a total ban on the kindly use of animals and natural resources; rather, it means putting an end to all forms of inhumanity and wanton destruction directed at animal life and the earth.

It is just such disregard that has made life desperate and painful for billions of animals worldwide. But today something can be done. This is the 1990s, after all—the environmental decade—and the habits and acts we claim as our own can either replenish or wreak havoc on the world. Indeed, by following the practical—and highly effective—suggestions in *You Can Save the Animals*, you will play a crucial role in preserving species, improving the quality of animal life, and obliterating animal suffering.

Some of the steps described in this activist's handbook are obvious. For instance, you can refrain from buying fur coats, refuse to hunt for recreation, and offer your home to a homeless animal.

But these steps are not enough. Virtually every aspect of your lifestyle, consuming habits, and community consciousness can be geared toward animal protection, as well. For example, you can let your lawn grow out so that your backyard becomes a meadow haven for a variety of displaced species. You can refuse to buy ivory, tortoiseshell ornaments, and even bone china—all made of animal parts. You can eat tuna only when it is sold by companies that don't catch dolphins in their nets. And you can avoid consuming meat and dairy products from animals bred in miserable, overcrowded, and disease-ridden factory farms.

The animal activist must also be an environmentalist. After all, saving the biosphere—the living earth—means fighting global warming and the greenhouse effect, which may engender mass extinctions; saving the oceans, where delicate ecosystems are carelessly destroyed and species from dolphins to whales are in danger of disappearing from the face of the earth; and protecting the rain forests, home to more than half of all plant, animal, and insect species.

Protecting the animals and the earth that they inhabit ultimately means getting politically involved. You may write to congressional representatives and companies to support laws and express views. (We make that easy for you by providing a list of addresses.) You may start local action committees. You can follow ten simple steps to pass animal protection laws in your area. You may even do something as provocative as buying up all the hunting permits for your local wildlife preserve and then throwing them out so that fewer "trophy" animals are killed.

Remember, half a century ago, Mahatma Gandhi said that the greatness of a nation could be judged by the "way in which its animals are treated." The spiritual insight of Francis of Assisi made him call all creatures our brothers and sisters. And as Albert Schweitzer advised, without a reverence for all life, we will never enjoy world peace.

What's more, as today's environmentalists point out, the future of the earth's animals will ultimately be our own. As we destroy their habitats, so we destroy our own environment and life-support systems. With 5.3 billion people on earth, we humans are simply too numerous to continue to live as predators—the planet is just too small. The human population now uses 40 percent of the world's resources. If our habits remain the same, and if, as predicted, our population doubles, we will leave precious few resources for ourselves—let alone for the other species of the earth. While overpopulation in the Third World is at crisis point, overconsumption in the developed world is no less serious. The average American child causes one hundred to two hundred times more harm to the earth then a child in India or Africa. So, we more fortunate people should consume less and have fewer children, too. A consumer society ultimately consumes itself.

By following the suggestions in *You Can Save the Animals*, you will make a significant contribution to the lives of animals worldwide. You will learn to fight the exploitation of lab animals, save elephants from being slaughtered for their ivory, prevent the needless destruction of insects, protect dolphins and whales, ease the plight of farm animals, enhance the lives of cats and dogs, and rescue thousands of endangered species. In the process, you will enhance your level of awareness and compassion and fight the scourge of overconsumption, linked to the disintegration of the atmosphere and the increasingly dysfunctional condition of the earth. We believe that if each human being would follow the steps in this simple handbook, the animals of the earth would truly be saved, and our own future and quality of life secured.

I

ANIMAL AWARENESS

Animal Sensitivity Training

■

One does not meet oneself until one catches the reflection from an eye other than human.

—Loren Eiseley

Any idea, person or object can be a Medicine Wheel, a mirror, for man. The tiniest flower can be such a mirror, a wolf, a story, a touch, a religion or a mountain top.

—Hyemeyohost Storm

To be a truly effective advocate for the animals of the earth, it is imperative that you be attuned to their lives. To start, we ask that you observe and understand animals, beginning with the animals you come in contact with every day. As you watch a variety of animals closely, ask yourself whether the creatures you are studying are governed by mindless instinct, or whether they seem to experience such emotions as affection and joy, anxiety and fear. Are they void of any real feeling, or do they actually seem to enjoy freedom, companionship, and other pleasures that we sometimes consider exclusively human?

As you begin to observe animals, including reptiles and insects, you will see that they are more like humans than you have ever thought. You will see that even though animals can't talk, as we do, they clearly express their emotional state, intentions, and expectations through expressive body language and sounds sometimes strikingly similar to our own. Note that both humans and dogs, for instance, may whine, growl, wimper, scream, or pant with excitement. Both humans and cats may purr with contentment. In fact, you will note that animals virtually always express their true feelings, while humans may often obscure their feelings with words.

Sit back and spend at least a half hour observing an animal you know relatively well. Note, for instance, how your dog seems to grin when greeting a loved one. See how your cat, much like you, scratches an itch and loves to eat tasty things. In fact, note how your pet communicates when it wants to be fed, played with, or taken for a walk. A dog that carries its leash as a signal that it wishes to leave is showing insight and reasoning—not just mechanical, conditioned reflex. Finally, take some time to observe a dog or cat as it sleeps. Notice how these animals will often twitch, whine, and move their limbs—clearly suggestive of the notion that they are having dreams and therefore have imaginations. (Watching a dog or cat play with a furry toy will also reveal their imaginative natures.)

Then, if possible, spend time observing animals that you don't come in contact with that often. Drive to a rural area and observe squirrels or deer; visit a local farm; or go to a local aquarium or zoo. Note the profound relationship between mothers and offspring. See the animals' drive for companionship. Sense the tranquility of animals in a natural setting. Note how many love to play and explore, investigating the world around them. And tune into the deep anxiety, even depression, exhibited by many animals in captivity, specifically those kept in inadequate, unnatural houses or cages.

Finally, observe some seemingly simple creatures like insects and worms. As you watch these animals, note how they express their will to live and avoid harm and injury. In fact, if you happen to witness insects drowning in a puddle or worms wriggling while being put on a fish hook, you will never again doubt their will to live. (Hopefully, you will feel enough empathy to come to the rescue.) It's no wonder that creatures exhibit so much angst: Scientists have recently found that when experiencing anxiety and fear, all bony fish, reptiles (including lizards, snakes, and turtles), amphibians (including frogs and salamanders), birds, and mammals produce the same type of neurochemicals as we do when terrified.

As you continue to observe and read more about a wide variety of animals, you will learn that some have powers far more developed than your own: Depending on the species, animals can see ultraviolet or infrared light; hear ultrasound; and even navigate by sensing magnetic fields or keeping track of the sun and stars.

After you have spent sufficient time observing a variety of species, please think about what you have learned. If you believe that people have souls, for instance, do you now feel that animals have souls as well? Do you feel that humans are superior to animals—an attitude that those in the animal-rights movement call "speciesism"—or just different? Do you believe that the difference you have observed is one of kind or one of degree? Do you feel a new sense of intimacy with other species?

Remember, the better you understand animal

behavior, the more you will enjoy the company of animals; recognize when one is sick and in need of veterinary care; intervene when you hear of cruel or indifferent treatment; and engender in your children a respect and reverence for all life.

2

Trading Places

■

First it was necessary to civilize man in relation to man. Now it is necessary to civilize man in relation to nature and the animals.
—Victor Hugo

To truly bond with animals, you can try to see the world through an animal's eyes. Toward that end, we suggest that you attempt "trading places," adapted from a series of interspecies communication exercises created by San Francisco experimental psychologist Keith Harary.

We would like to point out that the techniques and processes involved in trading places with animals are ancient indeed. The shamans and healers of our ancestral hunter-gatherer past wielded such techniques, often even taking their names (Black Elk, Eagle Man, *etc.*) from the animal kingdom. The practice of trading places with animals also helped skilled hunters of "sacred game." As the millennia passed, similar processes played a vital role in our ability to domesticate and husband animals with empathy and understanding. Versions of the technique are also instinctively tapped today by many

7

of our best farmers and veterinarians, who use intuition to help them in their trade.

Trading places with fellow creatures may seem to some modern folk like a kind of fantasy, an imaginative projection of the human mind alone. But that is not the case: It is, rather, a means of making an intuitive connection with creatures in the animal realm. Used to its fullest potential, this technique can help us all connect with animals that are, by and large, no longer a part of our lives—because most of us simply do not live close to nature, as did subsistence hunters of the past. Ending the separation between our species and others will mark the beginning of a more compassionate relationship between humans and the animals of the earth.

The best way to explore the Trading Places technique is to go for a drive to observe a bear, a deer, a coyote, or a horse—any animal that has a face. This exercise is also extremely well suited to scuba divers, who may practice underwater with many friendly forms of life. Finally, though we generally do not support the notion of keeping wild animals captive in zoos, for the purposes of this exercise you might also visit the most respected and humane zoo in your area. If the weather is forbidding, or if you are unable to make it out to the country or a zoo for any reason, you might also attempt this exercise with a house pet, or one or more birds in your yard.

If possible, we suggest that you spend a few hours or even a day closely observing as many animals as possible. A pair of binoculars is an asset. As you observe the activities of various animals, pay particular attention to the ways in which these creatures move and interact with fellow members of their species. Listen to their sounds, study the expressions that play across their faces and in their eyes, and observe their body language, postures, and displays. Also notice any special textures or smells. For instance, pay attention to the all-pervasive aroma of the lion house at the zoo, and to the slippery, shiny skin of the seal. As you study a number of animals, notice if there are any species with which you feel a special personal affinity. Do any animals remind you of yourself or your closest friend?

Your goal will be to choose an animal with whom you feel a particular affinity. For a few minutes, and possibly for as long as an hour, you will use visualization techniques to see yourself in that animal's place.

After you have chosen a special animal—be it your neighbor's dog, a grazing cow, or a monkey at the zoo—remember to be sensitive to that animal's needs. If you practice the Trading Places technique at the zoo, for instance, be sure to keep your distance; you might even select a time when the zoo isn't crowded and the animals are relatively calm.

Begin by choosing an animal with whom you feel at ease. Relax, and sit or stand in front of the creature that you have chosen so that you can look easily into each other's eyes. Do not do anything to make the animal nervous or tense. Do not, for instance, stare directly into the animal's eyes, because that can be perceived as a threat. Now take a deep breath. As you exhale slowly, look at the animal clearly, with an open mind, and push away all extraneous thoughts or distracting mental activities. As you continue to look at the animal, imagine that a part of your awareness is being transmitted through your breath into the animal's mind. At the same time, watch the animal breathe, and imagine that a part of its awareness is being transmitted into your mind.

Continue with this phase of the exercise for at

least five minutes, until you feel the boundaries between your identity and that of the animal becoming less rigid. As time goes on, you may find the sense of connectedness *so* intense that it feels powerfully real. You may also find yourself empathizing with the animal to such a large degree that it seems as if the two of you have mentally traded places. As the feeling of literally "trading places" sets in, imagine that you are looking out at the world from within the *animal's* body. Consider what you feel and what you see as you view the world from these new and unusual portals—your chosen animal's eyes.

If you have chosen your dog, imagine how this companion perceives its relationship to you and other humans; how it feels about its living conditions and its food; and what it perceives, feels, and anticipates from second to second in its journey through the world. If you have selected a caged lioness, experience her innate wildness—as well as the sense of loss she must feel at suppressing this wildness to survive within the artificial confines of the zoo.

After you have observed the world through the eyes of an animal for a while, shift your perspective so that your consciousness is centered back in yourself. As you gradually let go of the experience and return to your more familiar self, you should begin to recognize the parallels between the human and animal worlds. For instance, we and they all possess a will to live. (As Albert Schweitzer once advised, if you really want to know an animal—its inner essence, or soul, if you wish—you must attune your will-to-be with its will-to-be.) As a result of this exercise, you may even come to realize that the experience of trading places is a profound one for animals, too. It is through a similar process, after all, that companion animals often know that humans are sick or sad, and act gentler and more attentive in response. Finally, the Trading Places technique should help you understand that some animal traits, while *not* particularly human, are as valid and life-affirming as those that characterize the human realm.

After you have envisioned the world through one species, we suggest that you try the experiment with others. How does it feel to be a canary in a cage? A house cat in an animal shelter? A deer by the side of the highway? A squirrel in a tree? Does the world seem different to you as you trade places with a variety of creatures? Has "merging" with different species caused you to perceive reality in very different ways? Most important, please reflect upon the ways in which your empathy for, and perception of, animals has changed.

II
BETTER HOMES AND GARDENS

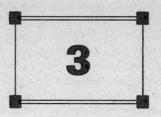

Create a Backyard Wildlife Habitat

We are part of the earth, and the earth is part of us. The fragrant flowers are our sisters; the reindeer, the horse, the great eagle, our brothers.

—Black Elk

Give up your lawn to nature. Let it go to seed—plant local wild flowers and create a meadow, providing a home and food for wild creatures.

To create a backyard wildlife habitat, first examine your yard or garden to see if any important habitat elements already exist. Look for plants that provide food, including seeds, fruits, and nuts; these things are important to such creatures as birds and squirrels. Also, see if you have a dense area of shrubbery or trees to provide cover for animals, protecting them from rain and wind and helping them escape from predators.

After you have assessed your yard for crucial habitat elements, take an inventory of everything else. First, list the names of the major cover plants (grasses, clovers, etc.), and also the name and size of every large shrub and tree in your yard. Then make a map showing where these plants are located in relation to everything else—including buildings, paths, pools, fences, and even rocks.

Now, using the skills that you gained during the "Trading Places" section of our guide, view your yard from the perspective of the animals. See that pile of dead brush? You had planned to remove it, but it *could* provide a wonderful home for a mother rabbit or field mouse that needs to bear and raise her young. Even a dead tree stump or log will provide food and a home for many creatures, from carpenter bees and ants to salamanders and snails.

After you have examined your yard for useful habitat elements, learn about the species that live in or pass through your area as part of a regular migration to other parts of the country. (For information about wildlife native to your region contact your Natural Wildlife Federation affiliate, the Department of Natural Resources, or the Department of Forestry, Fish, and Game Commission. You may also obtain information from your local library, nature center, or county extension service.) Decide which of these creatures you would be most interested in helping out, and go to it. For instance, if you want to share your space with butterflies, plant brightly colored flowers such as milkweed or butterfly bush. If you desire to share your space with birds, you might build an elevated birdbath to protect your guests from predators such as cats. If you would like some fish, frogs, or reptiles in your backyard, you can build a small ground pool; you will thus be providing drinking and bathing water for these creatures, and offering them cover for reproduction, as well.

No matter which species you decide to share your resources with, however, you must remember that *all* species require certain basic habitat elements. As you go about providing for the specific animals you have selected, do not forget these four requirements:

1. Food. Provide as much food as possible through natural vegetation. We suggest that you place particular emphasis on shrubs, trees, and other plants that provide nuts, berries, fruits, and seeds; these will meet the year-round needs of a large number of species, especially insects, which are, in turn, food for larger creatures. For specific recommendations about which plants to use, contact your local nature center or nursery. In the winter, you can supplement food provided by vegetation with sunflower seeds, proso millets, or cracked corn. Remember, if you set up a bird-feeding station, do not try to attract large numbers of birds by putting out a lot of seed. This could cause overfeeding, facilitate the spread of disease, and upset the birds' normal foraging or migratory behavior.

2. Water. All wildlife needs water for drinking and bathing. Depending upon the species you select, you may supply water through a birdbath, a small ground pool or clay dish, a waterfall, or a dripping hose. Whatever the source of water, it should be dependable year-round. In the summer, for instance, water evaporates and must be replaced regularly. During the winter, water freezes. You must remember to remove the ice and replenish the supply every day.

3. Cover. Just as you need clothes and a house, so, too, wildlife needs cover to protect it from the elements; to hide from predators; and to help conceive, bear, and raise the young. The best cover includes rock piles and stone walls, rotting logs, trees, man-made birdhouses, and a variety of plants, ranging from grass to dense shrubs to towering evergreens. We suggest that your backyard habitat contain a whole range of cover so that birds, small mammals, reptiles, and others may choose the type of cover they need.

You may also contact your local Audubon Society for details about putting up nesting boxes for rare local birds like the bluebird. If you have trouble locating your local branch, contact the National Audubon Society, P. O. Box 26666, Boulder, CO 80322.

One last tip: Please remember to make your backyard habitat hospitable to people, too. Shade trees, stretches of grass, and wooden benches will enable you to visit your personal wildlife refuge and commune with the animals for hours on end.

For a free brochure, entitled "Invite Wildlife to Your Backyard," write to the National Wildlife Federation, 1400 16th Street NW, Washington DC 20036.

To have your backyard certified as an official wildlife habitat, write to the National Wildlife Federation, Backyard Wildlife Habitat Program, 1400 16th Street NW, Washington, DC 20036-2266.

Take Your Garden Off Drugs

As cruel a weapon as the cave man's club, the chemical barrage has been hurled against the fabric of life.

—Rachel Carson

Visit any suburban neighborhood, and you're likely to see block after block of impeccably neat lawns. Where there was once a woodland, prairie, or meadow, hardly a creature stirs. The overriding reason: pesticides. One of the most important steps you can take in your effort to save the animals is to reject the use of insecticides and herbicides, which kill billions of innocent creatures—including birds, earthworms, and butterflies—each and every year. If you spray your lawn or garden with these toxic chemicals, you pose a grave danger to these smaller birds and animals, as well as to neighborhood children, cats, and dogs.

Indeed, it is ironic that more and more suburbanites want farmers to raise organic produce free of pesticides, yet these same people live in communities that often use more pesticide product per acre than most chemically dependent farmers.

If, like many suburbanites, you live in an area where manicured lawns and gardens are "de rigueur", you can still kick the chemical habit and control the onslaught of pets. For instance, you can reduce fungus outbreaks by improving air circulation in your garden; to do so, just thin and space plants, and remove parts that are diseased. If fungus continues to spread, you may avoid chemicals simply by washing plants off with a stream of water or a mild soapy solution. You can also learn about such plants as marigold and garlic, which help keep other plants near them free of pests.

We also suggest that, whether in your garden or home, you avoid the glue traps and fly paper often used to kill roaches, fruit flies, and a host of other insects. Creatures caught in these traps die slowly and horribly, unable to escape.

Finally, at all costs stay away from the patio bug zapper, one of the most indiscriminate forms of slaughter in suburbia. Patio bug-zappers consist of ultraviolet lights that attract insects and then electrocute them. Remember, insects that bite—mosquitoes, for instance—generally come out only in the early evening. Yet the bug zappers, which are generally left on twenty-four hours a day, kill all insects, including those that pollinate the flowers and serve as food for birds. To keep bugs away from you and your pets, we suggest a potent and completely safe insect repellant: lemon tea. To make, simply add a pint of boiling water to a chopped up lemon, let the mixture seep overnight, and apply as needed.

For further guidance, send for *How to Get Your Lawn and Garden Off Drugs*, published by Friends of the Earth, Suite 701, Laurier Avenue West, Ottawa, Ontario, Canada. Price: $10.50 (U.S.) including postage.

For any animal poison query or emergency, contact the National Animal Poison Information Network, University of Illinois/SRIB, 2004 Wright Street, Urbana IL 61801; 1-800-548-2433.

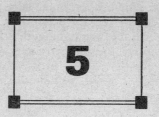

5

Make Your Home Pest-Proof

The most humane way to rid yourself of roaches, ants, silverfish, centipedes, earwigs, or any other flying or crawling insects in your home is to take great care to ensure cleanliness on all food surfaces. Do not leave dry dog food out; instead, keep it in the refrigerator or in a sealed container. Use caulking along baseboards and wherever the counter touches the edge of the wall so there are no places for roaches to nest. Check out your pipes and plumbing: There may be open spaces between the plumbing and the wall through which insects travel and in which they nest. To eliminate these problem spaces, stuff them with steel wool or some other appropriate material. If there are holes in your floorboards, fill them with sealant.

Since insects often get into the home through

windows, we suggest you make sure yours are bug-proof. If you do not have window screens, or if those in your home are damaged, it is time to add, repair, or replace them. Also, check out your porch. You might consider screening in your porch. If you leave your porch open, you should reject the conventional porch light in favor of a yellow bug light or citronella candles. The regular light attracts flying and crawling insects that can quickly get into your home. The yellow light, on the other hand, does not attract insects at all. Screen doors work well, too.

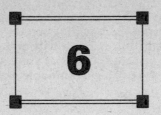

6

Use Humane Animal Traps

I am sometimes asked: Why do you spend so much of your time and money talking about kindness to animals when there is so much cruelty to men? I answer: I am working at the roots.

—George T. Angell

House mice, deer mice, and white-footed mice can gain access to your home or workplace through the smallest of openings. Once inside, they can feast on the food that you leave around and quickly multiply.

But you need not kill these animals in cruel and painful spring-activated traps or glue traps in order to get them out of your home. Instead, we suggest catching the mice in what's known as a "live-mouse trap"—one that catches the creatures but does not harm them—and then relocating these animals in an appropriate natural habitat. (Do not trap and relocate mice during the winter months; they will not survive the cold.)

We also suggest that you use live traps for wild creatures of any species at all—if their activities should conflict with yours to such a degree that they must be removed. No matter what the species, check your live trap every twelve hours. Do not set live traps during the breeding season, because babies separated from parents will certainly perish. Also, make sure that the animal you have caught is not a nursing female, identifiable through dark, distended nipples. If you have caught a nursing female, release her so that she can care for her young. Make sure to set the trap with food that will attract the specific species you are after. Also make sure to place the trap directly in the path of the animal that you desire to catch.

A guide to live traps, put together by the Humane Society of the United States, follows:

SOURCES OF LIVE-ANIMALS TRAPS

The following list is intended as a reference to firms manufacturing cage traps. No endorsement of specific brands is implied or intended. Cage traps may vary significantly in cost and performance.

The HSUS has excluded from this list the "Hava-hart Traps" manufactured by the Woodstream Corporation of Lititz, Pennsylvania. The Victor traps manufactured by this firm are the most widely used steel-jaw leghold traps in the United States. Steel-jaw leghold traps routinely cause injury and pain to animals. The HSUS supports state and federal bills to ban their use. The Woodstream Corporation provides financial assistance to commercial trappers in their campaigns against such legislation. Thus, the purchase of "Hava-hart Traps" may inadvertently, but directly, subsidize lobbying activities to perpetuate the use of cruel steel-jaw leghold traps.

"All Purpose Trap"
Ketch-All Company
2537 University Avenue
San Diego, CA 92104
(619) 297-1953

"Arrestor #3"
Stendal Products, Inc.
986 East Laurel Road
Bellingham, WA 98226
(206) 398-2353

"Hancock Beaver Trap"
Hancock Trap Company
Route 1, Box 38-2
Buffalo Gap, SD 57722
(605) 833-6530

"Mouse House"
Seabright Enterprises
  Ltd.
4026 Harlan Street
Emeryville, CA 94608
(415) 655-3126

"Mustang Live-Catch
  Traps"
Mustang Manufacturing
Company
P. O. Box 920947
Houston, TX 77292
(713) 682-0811

"National Live Traps"
National Live Trap
Corporation
Route 1, Box 302
Tomahawk, WI 54487
(715) 453-2249

"Safe-Sound Live
  Traps"
Meyer Manufacturing
Box 153
Garrison, IA 52229
(319) 477-5041
1-800-255-2255

"Sherman Small
  Mammal Live Traps"
H. J. Spencer & Sons
P. O. Box 131
Gainesville, FL 32602
(904) 372-4018

H. B. Sherman Traps,
  Inc.
P. O. Box 20267
Tallahassee, FL 32316
(904) 562-5566

"The Tender Trap"
Trap-Ease, Inc.
3001 Redhill Avenue
Building 4, Suite 120
Costa Mesa, CA 92626
(714) 979-5445

"Tomahawk Live Traps"
Tomahawk Live Trap
Company
P. O. Box 323
Tomahawk, WI 54487
(715) 453-3550

"Tru-Catch Traps"
Tru-Catch Traps
P. O. Box 816
Belle Fourche, SD
 57717
1-800-247-6132

A GUIDE TO CAGE TRAPS MADE TO CATCH COMMON WILDLIFE SPECIES

TRAP MANUFACTURER	beavers	cats (stray)	chipmunks	dogs (stray)	foxes	groundhogs	mice	muskrats	opossums	pigeons	rabbits	raccoons	rats	skunks	squirrels
Hancock Trap Co.	X														
H. B. Sherman Traps			X				X				X		X		X
Ketch-All Co.		X	X				X	X			X		X	X	X
Meyer Mfg.		X		X	X	X		X	X	X	X	X	X	X	X
Mustang Mfg.					X			X	X	X	X	X	X	X	X
National Live Trap Corp.	X	X	X	X	X	X	X	X	X	X	X	X	X	X	X
Seabright Enterprises							X								
H. J. Spencer & Sons							X						X		
Stendal Products		X							X					X	
Tomahawk Live Trap Co.	X	X	X	X	X	X	X	X	X	X	X	X	X	X	X
Trap-Ease, Inc.							X								
Tru-Catch Traps		X		X	X			X	X		X	X	X	X	X

HOW TO RELOCATE CAPTURED ANIMALS

Do not set mice free in the middle of an open field in broad daylight. (They may be devoured by predators.) Instead, we suggest relocating mice near dawn at least three hundred yards from your home (any closer, and they are likely to return), in areas with long grass or lush foliage.

As for other species, make sure to set the animal free in its home range, if at all possible. At worst, an animal released in completely unfamiliar surroundings may not survive; at best, it will be at a serious disadvantage in competing for food and living space. Make sure that the site at which you do release the animal constitutes a truly suitable habitat for that species. To make the best choice, seek advice from a game warden, park naturalist, or wildlife rehabilitator. Release any trapped animal with a stomach full of food; then arrange to provide food supplements for a few days to help the animal make the transition to its new home. Nocturnal species such as raccoons will have the best chance of survival if released at dusk. Squirrels and other diurnal (daytime) animals will do best released in the very early morning, just after dawn. Do not relocate animals during periods of excessive cold.

Make Your Home Wildlife-Proof

Woe to those who add house to house and join field to field until everything belongs to them and they are the sole inhabitants of the land.

—Isaiah

As our cities and towns spread, they often encroach into areas inhabited by wildlife. As a result, animals from bats and birds to squirrels and raccoons are displaced. Often, they seek shelter in attics, chimneys, garages, and other areas that seem, to them, the only viable substitute for their devastated home.

If you are one of the rare few who appreciates the sheer beauty of coexisting with wildlife, you may simply opt to let such animals share your home and do nothing. However, if you find yourself among the majority of people who would not enjoy having these creatures share your home, you may safeguard your property—and protect wild animals at the same time.

Indeed, all too often, people who find wild animals in their home deal with the problem by scaring, hurting, or killing the animals. This is not the way to go.

The best way to deal with the nuisance of wildlife in your house is to prevent these animals from entering in the first place. Toward that end, we suggest that you make your home secure sometime in the early fall. (If it turns out that animals have moved in, they will be less willing to leave in the spring, the season when offspring are born. In the winter, on the other hand, animals may be hibernating. In blocking entry to some animals, you may actually be trapping others inside.)

To make your home resistant to wildlife, start by fitting the chimney—a prime habitat for displaced birds—with a chimney cap. Also, check out your roof. If it is in disrepair, squirrels, bats, raccoons, and other creatures may get into your attic. You may also find birds building nests in kitchen and bathroom exhaust vents. Simply replace old vent covers with new ones. We suggest that you use covers with three or more shutter-type doors. Protect the entry to the vent pipe with a piece of wire mesh, and then attach the whole thing to the outside of your home with caulking. Garbage, of course, attracts wild animals, including cats and dogs. So try not to place your bags of garbage outside until the day they are to be collected. When your garbage does sit outside, make sure lids to cans are on tight. Finally, wildlife may sometimes build dens under houses and decks. To prevent this from happening, we suggest that you close these areas off by using prefabricated lattice or other materials.

By preventing unwanted wildlife from entering your home, you will be encouraging these animals to find safer—and more suitable—places to live.

Discard/Dispose with Care

The question is not, can they reason? Nor, can they talk? But can they suffer?

—Jeremy Bentham

Never discard the plastic harness that holds a six-pack of beer or soda without first cutting the loops with a pair of scissors or a knife. These six-pack holders have strangled thousands upon thousands of birds and small mammals. We also urge you to avoid the use of plastic whenever possible. Many manufacturers claim that their plastics are biodegradable, when this is not in fact so. (These plastics are only biodegradable in sunlight, which they are never exposed to in a landfill area.) Thus, they add to the destruction of the habitats and ecosystems of the earth.

One final tip: Do not, under any circumstance, participate in a balloon launch. Mylar balloons never decompose, and so-called biodegradable latex balloons take at least two months to start to decompose. The vast majority of these balloons come down over the ocean, where many are in-

31

gested by endangered sea turtles and other marine animals. The balloons block the creatures' intestines, resulting in death. Sea birds have also been found with ingested latex and have become entangled in the strings attached to the balloons.

All home and garden materials should be disposed of with great care. Separate garbage (glass, paper, metal, etc.) for recycling. Food—leftovers, leaves and lawn clippings make good compost for the garden. All chemicals (paint thinner, antifreeze, weed killer, etc.) should be sealed tightly for collection and not thrown out or poured down the drain.

III
FOOD FOR THOUGHT

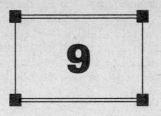

Eat Low on the Food Chain

■

It is my view that the vegetarian manner of living by its purely physical effect on the human temperament would most beneficially influence the lot of mankind.

—Albert Einstein

Consider what you eat. Decrease your consumption of meat by eating lower on the food chain—that is, eat less food of animal origin and more vegetables, fruits, and grains. As humans eat lower on the food chain, fewer animals will be subjected to the crowded, stressful, disease-ridden, often torturous life of the modern factory farm.

What's more, reducing the population of 1.2 billion cattle, 1.6 billion sheep and goats, and 800 million pigs is crucial to salvation of the earth. Indeed, like humans, these billions of farm animals waste massive quantities of natural resources and, because of all they consume, contribute to global warming, deforestation, soil erosion, and pollution of groundwater. Some 37 percent of the entire land mass of the United States is used to raise livestock. And the United Nations estimates that animal agriculture is responsible for 85 percent of topsoil loss, 260 million acres of U.S. forest destruction, and more than half of all water consumption. Animal agriculture daily pollutes groundwater with 20 billion pounds of manure. (Since animal feedstuffs are routinely mixed with such hazardous chemicals as arsenic-based compounds, copper, zinc, and selenium, manure that pollutes groundwater and topsoil has become one of the major impediments to a truly organic, sustainable agriculture in the United States today.) When you eat a portion of meat, you are, in essence, wasting twenty-five times the fossil fuel that you would use up had you consumed an equivalent amount of protein in grain. Finally, animal agriculture often eats up large quantities of wild lands, and thus literally exterminates wildlife.

Eating less meat is good for your health, too. High meat and animal-fat consumption is linked to breast cancer, colon cancer, cancer of the reproductive organs, osteoporosis, stroke, arteriosclerosis, and a host of other health problems.

You also may not be aware that, because slaughterhouse leftovers are voluminous, some factory farmers feed the remains of farm animals back to other farm animals. As a result, these naturally vegetarian creatures soon develop bacterial infections and cause food poisoning in the humans whose tables they reach.

We suggest you pick up a copy of *Diet for a New America,* by John Robbins. Walpole, N.H.: Stillpoint, 1986.

Also, look at *Organic Farmer Magazine: The Digest of Sustainable Agriculture,* 15 Barre Street, Montpelier, VT. 05602.

Go Vegetarian

I have from an early age abjured the use of meat, and the time will come when men such as I will look upon the murder of animals as they now look upon the murder of men.

—Leonardo da Vinci

If possible, we suggest that you become a true vegetarian. After all, the most effective way to save animals is simply to cease exploiting them in every possible way. A complete vegetarian diet is in your best interests from the standpoint of physical health, too. In fact, simply replacing meat with dairy products, fish, and seafood is not a wise choice. Dairy products tend to have a high fat content; milk often contains residues from chemicals and drugs. Government estimates that indicate that 50 percent of all dairy cows have mastitis, or udder infection, adds legitimacy to this concern. As for seafood, most is not subject to U.S. Department of Agriculture food-safety inspection. The oceans are liquid sewers: pesticides, heavy metals, and other industrial pollutants accumulate in the aquatic food chain, becoming concentrated in the tissues of fish, shrimp, crabs, and mollusks. In addition, commercially raised fish such as salmon and trout are generally raised in overcrowded conditions in floating enclosures or lagoons. The stress caused by such conditions drastically escalates the frequency of infection, making large doses of antibiotics and other drugs necessary. Such treatment puts consumers at risk and exposes large populations of free-ranging aquatic life to drug-contaminated water.

(Note: Please don't try to make your cat into a vegetarian. Cats are carnivores and need animal protein in their diets. Dogs are less carnivorous than cats, but don't put your dog on a vegetarian diet without first seeking good nutritional advice from a veterinarian.)

Useful books about the philosophy of vegetarianism include:

Akers, K. *A Vegetarian Source Book.* Arlington, VA: Vegetarian Press, 1983.

Altman, N. *Eating for Life.* Wheaton, IL: Theosophical Publishing House, 1973.

Dombrowski, D. A. *The Philosophy of Vegetarianism.* Amherst, MA: The University of Massachusetts Press, 1984.

Kapleau, P. *To Cherish All Life: A Buddhist View of Animal Slaughter and Meat Eating.* Rochester, NY: The Zen Center, 1981.

Lappé, F. M. *Diet for a Small Planet.* New York: Ballantine Books, 1971.

Rosen, S. *Food for the Spirit: Vegetarianism and World Religions.* New York: Bala Books, 1987.

Schwartz, R. H. *Judaism and Vegetarianism.* Smithtown, NY: Exposition Press, 1982.

Become a Conscientious Omnivore

No being likes to suffer. Therefore do not inflict suffering on any being. This is non–violence, this is equality.

—Jain Sutra Kratanga

If, like many people, you find it difficult to become totally vegetarian, declare yourself a conscientious omnivore and buy products from humanely and ecologically raised animals. Here are some guidelines:

• Check your local health-food store and farmer's market and buy organic, locally raised farm-animal produce. Many certified organic farmers practice relatively humane methods of raising animals for their milk, meat, and eggs. A guide to humane farms by region, compiled by The Humane Society of the U.S., appears below:

NORTHEAST REGION

Connecticut (CT)

Natural Organic Farmers Assn.-CT
Bill Duesing
Box 386, Northford, CT 06472
203/588-9280

CT Department of Agriculture
Kenneth B. Andersen,
  Commissioner
State Office Bldg., Hartford, CT
  06106
203/566-4667

Delaware (DE)

Eastern Shore Organic Directory
Sharon Carson
Rt. 2, Box 277, Delmar, DE 19940
*send $5.50 incl. postage for
  directory

DE Department of Agriculture
Michael R. Owens
2320 South Dupond Highway,
  Dover, DE 19901
302/726-4811

Maine (ME)

ME Organic Farmers & Gardeners
Nancy Ross
PO Box 2176, Augusta, ME 04338
207/622-3118

ME Department of Agriculture
Bernard A. Shaw, Commissioner
Statehouse Stn. 28, Augusta, ME
  04333
207/289-3810

Maryland (MD)

Eastern Shore Organic Directory
Sharon Carson
Rt. 2, Box 277, Delmar, DE 19940
*send $5.50 incl. postage for
  directory

MD Department of Agriculture
Wayne A. Cawley, Jr.
State House, Annapolis, MD 21401
301/974-3901

Massachusetts (MA)

Natural Organic Farmers Assn.-
  MA
Julie Rawson
RFD2 Shogun Rd., Barry, MA
  01005
508/355-2853

MA Dept. of Food & Agr.
August Schumacher, Jr.,
  Commissioner
Leverett Saltonstall Bldg., Gov't.
  Ctr.
100 Cambridge St., Boston, MA
  02202
617/727-3008

New Hampshire (NH)

Natural Organic Farmers Assn.-
  NH
Richard Estes
RFD1, Box 516, Andover, NH
  03216
603/648-2521

NHDA Certification Committee
Victoria Smith
10 Ferry St., Caller Box 2042,
  Concord, NH 03301
603/271-3685

New Jersey (NJ)

Natural Organic Farmers Assn.-NJ
Jennifer Morgan
RD #2, Box 263A, Pennington, NJ
  08534
609/737-3735

NJ Department of Agriculture
Arthur R. Brown, Jr.
CN 330, Trenton, NJ 08625
609/292-3976

New York (NY)

Natural Organic Farmers Assn.-
  NY
Pat Kane
PO Box 454, Ithaca, NY 14851
607/648-5557
*send $4.00 for "The Food Guide"

NY Dept. of Agr. & Markets
Richard T. McGuire,
  Commissioner
1 Winners Circle, Capital Plaza,
  Albany, NY 12235
518/457-4188

Pennsylvania (PA)

Biodynamic Farming &
  Gardening Assn.
Rod Shouldice
PO Box 550, Kimberton, PA 19442
215/935-7797

Organic Crop Improvement Assn.-
  PA
Ron Gargasz
RR #2, Box 116A, Volant, PA
  16156
412/530-7220

PA Department of Agriculture
Boyd E. Wolff
2301 North Cameron St.,
  Harrisburg, PA 17110-9408
717/787-4737

Rhode Island (RI)

Natural Organic Farmers Assn.-RI
Mike Merner
89 Country Dr., Charlestown, RI
  02813
401/364-9930

RI Dept. of Environmental
  Management
John M. Lawrence, III, Chief, Div.
  of Agr.
22 Hayes St., Providence, RI
  02908
401/277-2781

Vermont (VT)

Rural Vermont/Natural Organic
  Farmers Assn.-VT
Anthony Pollina
15 Barre St., Montpelier, VT
  05602
802/223-7222

VT Department of Agriculture
Ronald A. Allbee, Commissioner
116 State St., Montpelier, VT
  05602
802/828-2416

West Virginia (WV)

Mountain State Organic Growers
  & Buyers
Keith Dix
Route 10, Box 30, Morgantown,
  WV 26506
304/296-3978

WV Department of Agriculture
Cleve Benedict, Commissioner
State Capitol
Charleston, WV 25305
304/348-3550

NORTH CENTRAL REGION

Illinois (IL)

Organic Crop Improvement Assn.-
IN
Donna and Vaughn Edwards
RR 25, Box 218, Terre Haute, IN
47802
812/894-3143

IL Department of Agriculture
Larry A. Werries
St. Fairgrounds, PO Box 19281,
Springfield, IL 62794-9281
217/782-2172

Indiana (IN)

Organic Crop Improvement Assn.-
IN
Donna and Vaughn Edwards
RR 25, Box 218, Terre Haute, IN
47802
812/894-3143

IN Department of Agriculture
Doug Pond, Technical and
Financial Planning
IN Capitol, Ste. 600, Indianapolis,
IN 46204-2288
317/232-8770

Iowa (IA)

Organic Crop Improvement Assn.-
IA
Ken Rosmann
Rt. 1, Box 176, Harlan, IA 51537
712/627-4217

IA Organic Growers & Buyers
Allan Blair
Rt. 2, Box 130, Nichols, IA 52766
319/627-4217 (letters preferred)

IA Department of Agriculture and
Land Stewardship
Daryl Frey, Director of
Laboratory Div.
Henry A. Wallace Bldg., Des
Moines, IA 50319
515/281-8589

Kansas (KS)

KS Organic Producers
Judy Nickelson
PO Box 153, Beattie, KS 66406
913/353-2414

Organic Crop Improvement Assn.-
KS (East),
Joe Vogelsburg
RR 1, Home, KS 66438
913/799-3304

Organic Crop Improvement Assn.-
KS (East),
Ed Reznicek
RR 2, Box 23, Goff, KS 66428
913/939-2032

Organic Crop Improvement Assn.-
KS (West),
Leevern Koehn
HC1, Box 390, Sharon Springs,
KS 67758
913/852-4891

KS Board of Agriculture
Sam Brownback, Secretary
109 WE 9th St., Topeka, KS 66612
913/296-3556

Michigan (MI)

Organic Growers of MI
Lee Purdy
3928 South Sheridan, Lennon, MI
48449
313/621-4977

Organic Crop Improvement Assn.-
  MI
Tom Summers
3915 Dearing Rd., Parma, MI
  49269
517/788-7728

MI Department of Agriculture
Paul E. Kindinger, Director
PO Box 30017, Lansing, MI 48909
517/373-1104

Minnesota (MN)

Organic Growers and Buyers Assn.
Yvonne Buckley
1405 Silver Lake Rd., New
  Brighton, MN 55112
612/636-7933

MN Department of Agriculture
C. H. Eikenberry
90 W. Plato Blvd., St. Paul, MN
  55107
612/296-2627

Missouri (MO)

Ozark Organic Growers Assn.
  (NE)
Gregg Thorsen
Rt. 5, Box 1026, Ava, MO 65608
417/683-5109

Ozark Organic Growers Assn.
  (Spfld.)
Gary Jensen
1510 So. Jamestown Rd.,
  Springfield, MO 65809
417/865-0593

AR Small Farm Viability Project
Tim Snell
Rt. 2, Box 76, West Fork, MO
  72774
501/839-8218

Ozark Organic Growers Assn. (So.
  Central)
Mark Cain
Rt. 4, Box 158, Huntsville, MO
  72740
501/545-3558

MO Department of Agriculture
Charles E. Kruse, Director
PO Box 630, Jefferson City, MO
  65102-0630
314/751-3359

Nebraska (NE)

Organic Crop Improvement Assn.-
  NE
George Myers
4914 Ft. Kearney, Grand Island,
  NE 68801
308/382-2707

NE Department of Agriculture
George Beattie
PO Box 94947, Lincoln, NE 68509-
  4947
402/471-2341

North Dakota (ND)

Organic Crop Improvement Assn.-
  ND
Charles E. Wallace
RR 2, Box 79, Mott, ND 58646
701/563-4455

ND Department of Agriculture
Sarah Vogel, Commissioner
State Capitol, Bismarck, ND
  58505
701/224-2231

Ohio (OH)

OH Ecological Food & Farm Assn.
Holly Fackler
65 Plymouth St., Plymouth, OH
  44865
419/687-7665

Organic Crop Improvement Assn.-
  OH
David Baldock
328 N. Warren, Columbus, OH
  43204
614/279-3833

Organic Crop Improvement Assn.-
  Federation
Betty Kananen
3185 Township Rd., Bellefontaine,
  OH 43311
513/592-4983

OH Department of Agriculture
Steven D. Maurer, Director
65 S. Front St., Columbus, OH
  43215-4193
614/466-2732

South Dakota (SD)

Organic Crop Improvement Assn.-
  SD
Herb Allen
RD 2, Box 76A, Lake City, SD
  57247
605/448-5465

SD Department of Agriculture
Roger Scheibe, Director
445 E. Capitol, Pierre, SD 57501
605/773-3375

Wisconsin (WI)

Organic Crop Improvement Assn.-
  WI
Dan Patenaude
Rt. 1, Highland, WI 53543
608/929-7654

WI Organic Farmers
Faye Jones
Rt. 4, Box 104, Menomonie, WI
  54751
715/772-3104

WI Department of Agriculture,
  Agr. Res. Mgmt. Div.
Kenneth C. Rineer, Program
  Coordinator, Sustainable
  Agriculture
801 W. Badger Rd., PO Box 8911,
  Madison, WI 53708
608/267-3319

SOUTHERN REGION

Alabama (AL)

AL Department of Agriculture
Governor Guy Hunt
Governor's Office, Montgomery,
  AL 36130
205/242-7100

Arkansas (AR)

Ozark Organic Growers Assn.
Peggy Bonds
HCR 72, Box 35, Parthenon, AR
  72666
501/446-5604

Ozark Organic Growers Assn.
Keith Richards
PO Box 1211, Fayetteville, AR
   72702
501/521-0206

AR Industrial Development
   Commission
Clifton Meador, Director of Agr.
One State Capitol Mall, Little
   Rock, AR 72201
501/682-1121

Florida (FL)

FL Organic Growers, c/o Mark
   Ketchel
PO Box 365, High Springs, FL
   32645
904/454-4872
*send $2.50 for mailing directory

FL Department of Agriculture and
   Consumer Services
Doyle Conner, Commissioner
The Capitol, Tallahassee, FL
   32399-0810
904/997-2413

Georgia (GA)

GA Organic Growers Assn.
Larry Conklin
General Delivery, Madras, GA
   30254
404/621-4661 (leave message)

GA Department of Agriculture
Thomas T. Irvin, Commissioner
Agr. Bldg., Capitol Square,
   Atlanta, GA 30334
404/656-3685

Kentucky (KY)

KY Department of Agriculture
Ward Burnette, Commissioner
Capital Plaza Tower, Frankfort,
   KY 40601
502/564-4696

Louisiana (LA)

Krickhollow Farms, Dan
   Crutchfield
Rt. 1, Box 235, Jayess, MS 39641
601/684-4940
*supplies New Orleans market

MS Organic Growers Assn. (SE)
Alan Anderson
Rt. 2, Box 235, Poplarville, MS
   39470
601/795-2535
*supplies New Orleans market

LA Department of Agriculture and
   Forestry
Bryce Malone, Asst. Commissioner
Office of Marketing, PO Box 3334,
   Baton Rouge, LA 70821-3334
504/922-1277

Mississippi (MS)

MS Organic Growers Assn. (SE)
Tom Dana
Rt. 1, Box 442, Lumberton, MS
   39455
604/796-4406

MS Organic Growers Assn. (SE)
Alan Anderson
Rt. 2, Box 235, Poplarville, MS
   39470
601/795-2535

Krickhollow Farms, Dan
   Crutchfield
Rt. 1, Box 235, Jayess, MS 39641
601/684-4940

Rainbow Whole Foods (Jill/Liz/
   Bill)
4147 Northview Dr., Jackson, MS
   39206
601/366-1602

MS Department of Agriculture
and Commerce
Jim Buck Ross, Commissioner
PO Box 1609, Jackson, MS 39215-
1609
601/359-3634

North Carolina (NC)

Organic Crop Improvement Assn.-
NC
Brownie Van Dorp
Rt. 5, Box 262, Washington, NC
27889
919/946-7402

Carolina Farm Stewardship Assn.
Kate Havel
PO Box 511, Pittsborough, NC
27312
919/742-4672

NC Department of Agriculture
James A. Graham, Commissioner
Raleigh, NC 27611
919/733-7125

Oklahoma (OK)

Ozark Organic Growers Assn.
(NE)
Gregg Thorsen
Rt. 5, Box 1026, Ava, MO 65608
417/683-5109

Ozark Organic Growers Assn.
(Spfld.)
Gary Jensen
1510 So. Jamestown Rd.,
Springfield, MO 65809
417/865-0593

AR Small Farm Viability Project
Tim Snell
Rt. 2, Box 76, West Fork, MO
72774
501/839-8218

Ozark Organic Growers Assn. (So.
Central)
Mark Cain
Rt. 4, Box 158, Huntsville, MO
72740
501/545-3558

Ozark Organic Growers Assn.
Peggy Bonds
HCR 72, Box 35, Parthenon, AR
72666
501/446-5604

Ozark Organic Growers Assn.
Keith Richards
PO Box 1211, Fayetteville, AR
72702
501/521-0206

OK Department of Agriculture
Jack D. Craig, Commissioner
2800 North Lincoln Blvd.,
Oklahoma City, OK 73105-4298
405/521-3864

South Carolina (SC)

SC Organic Assn.
Margaret Locklear
129 Organic Lane, W. Columbia,
SC 29169
803/791-5733

SC Department of Agriculture
Governor Carroll A. Campbell, Jr.
Office of the Governor, Office of
Exec. Policy & Programs
1205 Pendleton St., Columbia, SC
29201
803/734-2210

Tennessee (TN)

TN Alternative Growers Assn.
Shannon Stoney
2802 Brangus Lane, Cookeville,
TN 38501
615/537-9432

TN Department of Agriculture
L.H. Ivy, Commissioner
Ellington Agr. Ctr., Nashville, TN
  37204
615/360-0103

Texas (TX)

TX Organic Growers Assn.
Shirley Fraizer
Rt. 1, Box 419, Welder, TN 78959
512/540-4881

TX Department of Agriculture
Keith Jones, Organic Program
  Specialist
PO Box 12847, Austin, TX 78711
512/463-9883

Virginia (VA)

Rural VA
Rick Cagan
Box 252, Flint Hill, VA 22627
804/353-8683

VA Assn. of Biological Farmers
Patti Nesbit-Habib
PO Box 2766, Charlottesville, VA
  22902
703/636-1817
*send $10.00 for directory

Eastern Shore Organic Directory
Sharon Carson
Rt. 2, Box 277, Delmar, DE 19940
*send $5.50 incl. postage for
  directory

VA Department of Agriculture
S. Mason Carbaugh,
  Commissioner
PO Box 1163, Richmond, VA
  23209
804/786-3501

WESTERN REGION

Alaska (AK)

AK Division of Agr.
Frank Mielke, Director, Dept. Nat.
  Res.
915 S. Bailey, Palmer, AK 99645-
  0949
907/745-7200

California (CA)

California Certified Organic
  Farmers (Central Office)
Mark Lipson
PO Box 8136, Santa Cruz, CA
  95061
408/423-2263

CA Department of Food and
  Agriculture
Jed A. Adams
1220 N. St., PO Box 942871,
  Sacramento, CA 94271-0001
916/445-2491

Colorado (CO)

CO Organic Producers Assn.
Tom Hamilton
23242 Highway 371, La Jara, CO
  81140
719/274-5230

CO Department of Agriculture
Steven W. Horn, Commissioner
1525 Sherman St., Denver, CO
  80203
303/866-2811

Hawaii (HI)

HI Board of Agriculture
Yukio Kitagawa, Chairperson
PO Box 22159, Honolulu, HI
  96822-0159
808/548-7101

Idaho (ID)

ID Organic Producers Assn.
Tim Sommer
11741 Bullock Lane, Middleton,
  ID 83701
208/334-3240

ID Department of Agriculture
Rick Phillips
PO Box 790, Boise, ID 83701
208/334-3240

Montana (MT)

Organic Crop Improvement Assn.-
  MT (North Central)
Bob Quinn
Round River Ranch, Box 808, Big
  Sandy, MT 59520
406/378-3105

Organic Crop Improvement Assn.-
  MT (NE)
Dewey Forsness
Box 5035, Wolf Point, MT 59201
406/653-2492

Alternative Energy Resource Org.
Nancy Matheson
44 North Last Chance Gulch,
  Helena, MT 59601
406/443-7272

MT Dept. of Health and
  Environmental Science
Larry Lloyd
Cogswell Bldg., Helena, MT 59620
406/444-2408

Nevada (NV)

NV Department of Agriculture
Thomas W. Ballow, Exec. Dir.
PO Box 11100, Reno, NV 89510-
  1100
702/789-0180

New Mexico (NM)

Organic Crop Improvement Assn.-
  NM
Carol Underhill
Talavaya Center, Espanola, NM
  87537
505/685-4577

NM Department of Agriculture
Governor G. Carruthers
Box 30005, Dept. 3189, Las
  Cruces, NM 88003-0005
505/646-3007

Oregon (OR)

OR Tilth Provender
Yvonne Frost
PO Box 218, Tualatin, OR 97062
503/692-4877
*send $10.00 for directory

OR Department of Agriculture
W. H. Kosesan, Deputy Director
635 Capitol St., NE, Salem, OR
  97310-0110
503/378-4665

Utah (UT)

UT Department of Agriculture
Miles Ferry, Commissioner
350 North Redwood Rd., Salt
  Lake City, UT 84116
801/538-7100

Washington (WA)

Tilth Producers Cooperative
Anne Schwartz
1219 East Sauk Rd., Concrete, WA
  98237
206/853-8449

WA Department of Agriculture
C. Alan Pettibone, Director
406 General Admin. Bldg., AX-41,
  Olympia, WA 98504-0641
206/753-5042

Wyoming (WY)

WY Department of Agriculture
Don Rolston, Commissioner
Cheyenne, WY 82002-0100
307/777-7321

• Boycott factory-farm pork products. Breeding sows, used to produce the piglets ultimately fattened into pork, ham, and bacon, undergo extreme abuse. On the modern factory farm, rows of sows are housed indoors, often in semidarkness, on concrete slabs without bedding. For several years running, they are either chained to the ground with a collar around their necks or shoulders, or are kept in narrow stalls in which they cannot even turn around.

• Eat eggs only from free-range chickens. On the modern factory farm, laying hens are stuffed into tiny battery cages. Overcrowded, chronically stressed, and frequently cannibalized, they often collapse because of soft bones that have been depleted of minerals and wind up in chicken pot-pies, soups, and pet food.

• Never eat veal from special "milk-fed" veal calves. For sixteen weeks on end, these animals are kept in social isolation in individual wooden crates so narrow that they cannot turn around, make normal postural adjustments, or even groom themselves properly. The calves are kept relatively immobilized so that their meat will be tender, like newborn baby veal. Since the highest-priced meat must also be white, the calves are deprived of hay and other natural roughage that contains iron. This renders them borderline anemic. Many calves are literally cripples and have great difficulty walking when uncrated and driven into trucks to go to the slaughterhouse.

■━━━━━━━━━━━━━━━━━━━━━━━━━━━━━━━━━━━■

To set up a local action group so that you can spread the word about eating with a conscience, contact *Earthsave*, 706 Frederick Street, Santa Cruz, CA 95062-2205; (408) 423-4069.

■━━━━━━━━━━━━━━━━━━━━━━━━━━━━━━━━━━━■

12

Become a Vegetarian Epicure

■

Nothing more strongly arouses our disgust than cannibalism, yet
we make the same impression on Buddhists and vegetarians, for we
feed on babies, though not on our own.

—Robert Louis Stevenson

Whether or not you have decided to go completely
vegetarian, buy some vegetarian cookbooks and try
some healthy and environmentally safe recipes.

■━━━━━━━━━━━━━━━━━━━━━━━━━━━━━━━━■

A few excellent guide books to becoming a vegetarian gourmet
include:

Brooks, Karen. *The Complete Vegetarian Cookbook*. New York:
    Pocket Books, 1974.
Ewald, Ellen Buchman. *Recipes for a Small Planet*. New York:
    Ballantine Books, 1973.
Hagler, Louise. *The Farm Vegetarian Cookbook*, edited by Louise
    Hagler (available from The Book Publishing Company, 156 Drakes
    Lane, Summertown, TN 38483; all-Vegan recipes).
Katzen, Mollie. *The Moosewood Cookbook*. Berkeley, CA: Ten Speed
    Press, 1977.

————. *The Enchanted Broccoli Forest*. Berkeley, CA: Ten Speed Press, 1982.

McClure, Joy, and Layne, Kendall. *Cooking for Consciousness*. Denver: Ananda Marga Publications, 1976.

Robertson, Laurel, Flinders, Carol, and Godfrey, Bronwen. *Laurel's Kitchen: A Handbook for Vegetarian Cookery and Nutrition*. Petaluma, CA: Nilgiri Press, 1976.

Thomas, Anna. *The Vegetarian Epicure*. New York: Vintage Books, 1972.

————. *The Vegetarian Epicure, Book Two*. New York: Alfred A. Knopf, 1981.

World of God. *The Cookbook for People Who Love Animals*. P. O. Box 1418, Umatilla, FL 32784, 1983 (all-Vegan recipes).

You may also wish to subscribe to *Vegetarian Times* magazine and purchase their excellent *Vegetarian Times Cookbook* (P.O. Box 466, Mt. Morris, IL 61054-9894).

If you are seeking vegetarian recipes for an institutional setting such as a hospital or school, contact the Physicians Committee for Responsible Medicine, P. O. Box 6332, Washington, DC 20015.

Eat Dolphin-Safe Tuna

Now I can look at you in peace; I don't eat you anymore.
—Franz Kafka

Three years ago, California biologist Sam LaBudde went undercover, taking a job as a cook on a tuna vessel. While on board, he videotaped dolphins getting caught and killed in fishing nets along with schools of yellowfin tuna. His footage lent powerful proof—and new fervor—to assertions that large numbers of dolphins were being slaughtered in tuna nets every time tuna boats went out. (Experts estimated the death rate at 100,000 a year.)

Though the tuna industry had long ignored the protest, this time the evidence was just too strong. In April 1990, animal-rights activists, conservationists, and consumers were finally rewarded with a positive industry response. First, the Pittsburgh-based H. J. Heinz Co., which owns the Star Kist brand of tuna, announced that it would stop buying tuna caught in nets that also trap dolphins. Later the same day, Van Camp Seafood Company, which markets Chicken of the Sea, followed suit. Those concerned about dolphins should buy tuna only from these companies and any others whose tuna is labeled dolphin-safe.

Two further notes: Despite positive action on the part of a few companies, the threat posed by the fishing industry to dolphins, porpoises, small whales, and other cetaceans is grave. The Environmental Investigation Agency (EIA), a London-based

---

Feed Your Conscience

The following directory will guide you to healthy, animal-friendly sources of food.

Americans for Safe Food/Center for Science in the Public Interest, 1501 16th Street, NW, Washington, DC 20036; (202) 332-9110. National coalition of consumer, environmental, and farm organizations publishes a list of eighty-five mail-order suppliers of organic foods.

Co-op America Alternative Catalogue, Catalogue Services Dept., 126 Intervale Road, Burlington, VT 05401; (802) 658-5507.

EccoBella, 6 Provost Square, Suite 602, Caldwell, NJ 07006; (201) 226-5799 (biodegradable plastics, etc.).

Healthy Harvest II: A Directory of Sustainable Agriculture and Horticulture Organizations, Potomac Valley Press, 1424 16th Street, NW, Suite 105, Washington, DC 20036. Lists organizations, publications, and retailers working to make our food supply safer and our agricultural methods more environmentally sound.

Seventh Generation Catalogue, 126 Intervale Road, Burlington, VT 05401; (802) 862-2999.

Shopper's Guide to Natural Foods: A Consumer's Guide to Buying and Preparing Foods for Good Health, Avery Publishing Group, Inc., Garden City Park, NY 11040. A guide of the "healthiest" food in the supermarket or natural-food store.

Shopping for a Better World Catalogue, Council on Economic Priorities, 30 Irving Place, New York, NY 10003; (800) U-CAN-HELP; (212) 420-1133 in New York.

conservation group, estimates that tens of thousands of these marine mammals are needlessly killed by fishermen each year. According to estimates, half a million of these mammals are slaughtered yearly by the fishing industry worldwide.

You may want to think twice about eating shrimp because thousands of sea turtles drown in shrimp fishing nets and far from all shrimp fishermen use Turtle Extruder Devices that help keep these ancient and endangered species out of the nets.

IV
THE COMPASSIONATE CONSUMER

14

Use Animal-Friendly Household Products and Cosmetics

■

. . . it is difficult to picture the great Creator conceiving of a program of one creature (which He has made) using another living creature for purposes of experimentation. There must be other, less cruel ways of obtaining knowledge.

—Adlai Stevenson

Ask the experimenters why they experiment on animals, and the answer is: "Because the animals are like us." Ask the experimenters why it is morally okay to experiment on animals, and the answer is: "Because the animals are not like us." Animal experimentation rests on a logical contradiction.

—Charles R. Magel

I had bought two male chimps from a primate colony in Holland. They lived next to each other in separate cages for several months before I used one as a [heart] donor.

When we put him to sleep in his cage in preparation for the operation, he chattered and cried incessantly. We attached no significance to this, but it must have made a great impression on his companion, for when we removed the body to the operating room, the other chimp wept bitterly and was inconsolable for days.

The incident made a deep impression on me. I vowed never again to experiment with such sensitive creatures.

—Christian Barnard

If we cut up beasts simply because they cannot prevent us and
because we are backing our own side in the struggle for existence,
it is only logical to cut up imbeciles, criminals, enemies, or capital-
ists for the same reasons.

—C. S. Lewis

Avoid the use of cosmetics, detergents, cleaning
fluids, and other chemicals that have been point-
lessly tested on laboratory animals or that make
use of animal products. (These are usually the same
products that are environmentally harmful, as
well.) Many soaps, for instance, contain tallow obtained from cats and dogs housed at shelters, ex-
hausted dairy cows, and overfed chickens and pigs.
New household products are frequently tested on
animals, who suffer and die so that some trivial
innovation may be proved safe for human use.
Numerous name-brand cosmetics companies also
regularly test their mascaras, eye liners, and skin
creams on rabbits, rats, and mice.

Three Common Animal Tests

THE DRAIZE EYE-IRRITANCY TEST

Generally conducted on rabbits, the Draize Eye-Irritancy Test is used
to estimate how damaging a particular substance is to the human eye.
First the test rabbits are restrained. Then test substances are placed in
their eyes. Depending upon the irritancy of the substance, the rabbits
experience anything from mild redness to swelling to ulceration to
outright bleeding.

Not only is the Draize Eye-Irritancy Test painful, sometimes unbear-
ably so, but it is also unreliable. The researcher conducting the test,
after all, determines the so-called irritancy of the substance simply by
studying the rabbit's eye. Thus, the outcome is subjective, varying
from tester to tester. What's more, even when all agree that the

substance has irritated the rabbit's eye, it still may not irritate the human eye. On the other hand, a substance that has not affected the rabbit's eye may be quite disruptive in the human counterpart.

THE DRAIZE SKIN-IRRITANCY TEST

Like the Draize Eye-Irritancy Test, the Skin-Irritancy Test exposes the shaved skin of rabbits or guinea pigs to test substances. Again, researchers examine the degree of swelling, ulceration, and bleeding to determine the irritancy of the product, cosmetic, or drug.

THE LD-50 TEST

The LD in the name of the LD-50 test stands for "lethal dose." The aim of the LD-50 Test is to determine just how poisonous a particular substance may be to humans. To perform the test, researchers force a group of animals—usually mice or rats—to ingest the substance until 50 percent of them die. As the test substance takes effect, signs of poisoning include bleeding from the eyes, nose, and mouth; labored breathing; convulsions and tremors; paralysis; and, ultimately, coma. Those animals not killed by the substance after two weeks are put to death by the tester.

Not only does the LD-50 Test constitute cruel and unusual punishment; it is also virtually useless in predicting doses lethal to humans.

Though still performed by many corporations (see listing on page 63), these tests are not required by law. And with good reason: In one frequently cited lawsuit, a judge ruled that the plaintiff had not shown that "the results of tests on rabbit eyes can be extrapolated to humans." In other words, testing on animals does not legally guarantee a product's safety.

Ethical insights are born in attacks upon conformity to existing mores.

—Rollo May

There are a number of alternatives to animal testing. They include:

- No test at all for products made from natural, well-known ingredients.
- Test-tube procedures, which use cells, tissue fragments, and organs. These cell cultures, derived from humans, are often more accurate than tests on animals in showing just how the human being will react. Experimenters using test-tube techniques can also test substances directly on human eye tissue derived from eye banks and eye research centers.
- Chemical tests, such as the Eytex Test. This test, available as a kit from a California firm, contains chemicals that turn cloudy when irritants are added—just like the eye itself responds.
- Tests on non-sentient beings that feel no pain, such as single-cell organisms. One promising alternative includes the use of chick embryos, which do not yet have the capacity to feel pain—but do have an outer membrane that responds to irritants much the same as the human eye does.
- Computer models. A number of computer programs can now predict how irritating a chemical is likely to be, based on its chemical and physical properties.

To be an animal-friendly consumer, stick to old—and already tested—brands of cleaning agents, toiletries, and non-prescription drugs. Do not support the killing of thousands of rabbits by buying some new, "improved," marginally different mouth wash or eye wash. Indeed, sticking to old brands will help reduce industry's incentive to use and abuse more animals in researching and developing new, nonessential products. Finally, if you do try a new product, make sure it is manufactured by one of the companies that now rejects animal testing and animal exploitation in any form.

After you have decided to use only animal-friendly products, explain your actions to your friends. Let them know about the cruelty-free alternatives to the products they use, and ask local merchants to carry these brands.

Most of the time, you will be able to find cruelty-free products at health-food stores, food cooperatives, and even mixed in with the stock at many supermarkets and drugstores. However, if you have trouble finding a product not tested on or exploitive of animals, you can tap the following resource guide, supplied by the Humane Society of the United States.

COMPANIES THAT MANUFACTURE PRODUCTS NOT TESTED ON ANIMALS

The following companies identified by The Humane Society of the United States manufacture products that are not tested on animals:

Abracadabra, Inc., P. O. Box 1040, Guerneville, CA 95446; (707) 869-0761

Aditi Nutri-Sentials, P. O. Box 155, New York, NY 10012; (212) 533-6962

African Bio-Botanica Industries, Inc., 7509 B NW 13th Boulevard, Gainesville, FL 32606; (904) 376-7329/7679

Alba Botanica Cosmetics, P. O. Box 1858, Santa Monica, CA 90406; (213) 451-0936

Alexandra Avery, Northrup Creek, Clatskanie, OR 97016; (503) 755-2446

Allens Naturally, P. O. Box 514, Farmington, MI 48332-0514; (313) 453-5410

Aloegen (*see* Levlad, Inc.)

Alva-Amco Pharmacal Companies, Inc., 6625 Avondale Avenue, Chicago, IL 60631; (312) 792-0200

American Merfluan, Inc., 41 Sutter Street, Suite 1153, San Francisco, CA 94104; (415) 387-2620

Amway Corporation, 7575 Fulton Street East, Ada, MI 49355-0001; (616) 676-6279

Andalina, Tory Hill, Warner, NH 03278-0057; no telephone listed

Aroma Vera Company, 2728 South Robertson Boulevard, Los Angeles, CA 90034; (231) 280-0407

Atta Latti, 443 Oakhurst Drive, #305, Beverly Hills, CA 90212; (213) 274-8840

Attitudes Unlimited (*see* Image Laboratories, Inc.)

Aura Cacia, P. O. Box 3157, Santa Rosa, CA 95402; (707) 584-5115

Auromere, 1291 Weber Street, Pomona, CA 91768; (714) 629-8255

Autumn-Harp, Inc., 28 Rockydale Road, Bristol, VT 05443; (802) 453-4807

Avanza Corp. (*see* Nature Cosmetics, Inc.)

Aveda, 321 Lincoln Street NE, Minneapolis, MN 55413; (612) 379-8500

Aztec Herbs (*see* Michael's Naturopathic Programs)

Baby Touch, Ltd., 100 Sandpiper Circle, Corte Madera, CA 94925; no telephone listed

Bare Escentuals, 104 Cooper Court, Los Gatos, CA 95030; (408) 354-8853

Beauty Without Cruelty, Ltd./Pamela Marsen, Inc., 451 Queen Anne Road, Teaneck, NJ 07666; (201) 836-7820

Bio-Nature International (*see* Martin Von Myering, Inc.)

Blackmore's, 16 Parkside Drive, North Burnswick, NJ 08902; (201) 422-7440

Body Love, P. O. Box 7542, Santa Cruz, CA 95061; (408) 425-8218

The Body Shop, Inc., 45 Horsehill Road, Hanover Technical Center, Cedar Knolls, NJ 07927-2003; (201) 984-9200, or 1-800-541-2535

Borlind of Germany, P. O. Box 1487, New London, NH 03257; (603) 526-2076

Botanicus, 7920 Queenair Drive, Gaithersburg, MD 20879; (301) 977-8887, or 1-800-282-8887

Chenti Products, Inc., 21093 Forbes Avenue, Hayward, CA 94545; (415) 785-2177

Christian Dior Perfumes, Inc., 9 West 57th Street, New York, NY 19153; (212) 759-1840

Clientele, 5207 NW 163rd Street, Miami, FL 33014; (305) 624-6665

Come to Your Senses, Inc., 321 Cedar Avenue South, Minneapolis, MN 55454; (612) 339-0050

Comfort Manufacturing Co., 1056 West Van Buren Street, Chicago, IL 60607; (312) 421-8145

Community Soap Factory, P. O. Box 32057, Washington, DC 20007; (202) 347-0186

Country Comfort, 28537 Nuevo Valley Drive, P. O. Box 3, Nuevo, CA 92367; (714) 657-3438

Crabtree & Evelyn, Ltd., Peake Brooke Road, P. O. Box 167; Woodstock, CT 06281; (203) 928-2761

Creme De La Terre, 24 Calhoun Drive, Greenwich, CT 06831; no telephone listed

Dermelle (*see* Essque Bodycare)

Desert Essence Cosmetics, P. O. Box 588, Topanga, CA 90290; (213) 455-1046

D+P Products, Inc., P. O. Box 5601, 2810 East Long Street, Tampa, FL 33605-5601; (813) 248-6640

Dr. Bronner's, P. O. Box 28, Escondido, CA 92025; (619) 743-2211

Earth Science, P. O. Box 1925, Corona, CA 91718; (714) 630-6720

Ecco Bella, 125 Pompton Plains Crossroads, Wayne, NJ 07470; (201) 890-7077

Espree Cosmetics, P. O. Box 160249, Irving, TX 75016; (214) 929-4425

Essque Bodycare, P. O. Box 7635, Greenwich, CT 06836; (203) 322-8778

European Soaps, 12300 15th Avenue NE, Seattle, WA 98125; (206) 361-9143

Eve Cosmetics, P. O. Box 131, Pebble Beach, CA 93953; no telephone listed

Fabergé, Inc., 725 Fifth Avenue, New York, NY 10022; (212) 735-9300

Fashion Two Twenty, Inc., 1263 South Chillicothe Road, P. O. Box 220, Aurora, OH 44202; (216) 562-5111

4-D Hobe Marketing Corp., 201 South McKemy, Chandler, AZ 85226; (602) 257-1950

Fruit of the Earth, Inc., P. O. Box 727, Bensenville, IL 60106; (312) 766-5400

A. J. Funk and Co., 1471 Timber Drive, Elgin, IL 60120; (312) 741-6760

Giovanni Cosmetics, Inc., P. O. Box 39378, Los Angeles, CA 90039; (213) 663-7033

Golden Pride/Rawleigh, 1107 Lake Avenue, Lake Worth, FL 33460; (407) 586-7778

Golden Star, Inc., 400 East 10th Avenue, P. O. Box 12539, North Kansas City, MO 64116; (816) 842-0233

Gruene, Inc., 1621 West Washington Boulevard, Venice, CA 90291; (213) 392-2449

G. T. International, 1800 South Robertson Boulevard, Suite 182, Los Angeles, CA 90035; (213) 551-0484

Hair Muscle (*see* Image Laboratories, Inc.)

Hawaiian Resources Co., Ltd., 1123 Kapahulu Avenue, Honolulu, HI 96816; (808) 737-8726

Heavenly Soap, 5948 East 30th Street, Tucson, AZ 85711; (602) 790-9938

Home Health Products, Inc., P. O. Box 3130, Virginia Beach, VA 23454; (804) 491-2200

Home Service Products Co., 230 Willow Street, Bound Brook, NJ 08805; (201) 356-8175

Humane Alternative Products, 8 Hutchins Street, Concord, NH 03301; (603) 228-1929

Humphreys Pharmacal, Inc., P. O. Box 256, 63 Meadow Road, Rutherford, NJ 07070; (201) 933-7744

Ida Grae Products (*see* Nature's Colors Cosmetics)

Ilona of Hungary, Inc., 3201 East 2nd Avenue, Denver, CO 80206; (303) 320-5991

Image Laboratories, Inc., P. O. Box 55016, Metro Station, Los Angeles, CA 90055; (213) 623-9254

Inner Health Herbs (*see* Michael's Naturopathic Programs)

Institute of Trichology, 1619 Reed Street, Lakewood, CO 80215; (303) 232-6149

International Rotex, Inc., P. O. Box 20697, Reno, NV 89515; (702) 356-8356

Internatural, P. O. Box 463, South Sutton, NH 03273; (603) 927-4776

Jason Natural Products, Inc., 8468 Warner Drive, Culver City, CA 90232-2484; (213) 838-7543

Jeanne Rose Herbal Body Works (*see* New Age Creations)

John Paul Mitchell Systems, P. O. Box 10597, Beverly Hills, CA 90213-3597; (818) 407-0500

Jurlique Cosmetics, 16 Starlit Drive, Northport, NY 11768; (516) 754-3535

Kallima International, 915 Whitmore, Rockwall, TX 75087; (214) 771-0011

Kimberly Sayer Skin Care System, 61 West 82nd Street, Suite 5A, New York, NY 10024; (212) 362-2907

Kiss My Face Corp., P. O. Box 804, New Paltz, NY 12561; (914) 255-0884

KMS Research Laboratories, Inc., 6807 Highway 299 East, Bella Vista, CA 96008; (916) 549-4472

KSA Jojoba, 19025 Parthenia Street, Northridge, CA 91324; (818) 701-1534

Lady Finelle Cosmetics, 137 Marston Street, P. O. Box 5200, Lawrence, MA 01842-2808; (617) 682-6112

L'Anza Research International, Inc., 5523 Ayon Avenue, Irwindale, CA 91706; (818) 334-9333

Levlad, Inc., 9183-5 Kelvin Avenue, Chatsworth, CA 91311; (818) 882-2951

Lily of the Desert, 2001 Walnut Hill Lane, Irving, TX 75038; (214) 518-0612

Lily of Colorado, 1286 South Valentia Street, Denver, CO 80231; (303) 455-4194

Livos Plant Chemistry, 2641 Cerrillos Road, Santa Fe, NM 87501; (505) 988-9111

Magic American Corp., 23700 Mercantile Road, Cleveland, OH 44122; (216) 464-2353

Marie Lacoste Enterprises, Inc., 1059 Alameda de Las Pulgas, Belmont, CA 94002; (415) 361-1277

Martin Von Myering, Inc., 422 Jay Street, Pittsburgh, PA 15212; (412) 323-2832

Merle Norman Cosmetics, 9130 Bellanca Avenue, Los Angeles, CA 90045; (213) 641-3000

Michael's Naturopathic Programs, 7050 Alamo Downs Parkway, San Antonio, TX 78238; (512) 647-4700

Micro Balanced Products, 25 Alladin Avenue, Dumont, NJ 07628; (201) 387-0200

Mira Linder Spa in the City, 29935 Northwestern Highway, Applegate Square, Southfield, MI 48034; (313) 356-5810

Mountain Ocean, Ltd., P. O. Box 951, Boulder, CO 80306; (303) 444-2781

Natural Research People, Inc., South Route, P. O. Box 12, Lavina, MT 59046; (406) 575-4343

Nature Cosmetics, Inc., 881 Alma Real, Suite 101, Pacific Palisades, CA 90272; (213) 459-9816

Nature's Colors Cosmetics, 424 Laverne Avenue, Mill Valley, CA 94941; (415) 388-6106

Nature's Gate Herbal (see Levlad, Inc.)

Nectarine (see Terra Nova)

New Age Creations, 219 Carl Street, San Francisco, CA 94117; (415) 564-6785

New Age Products, 16100 North Highway 101, Willits, CA 95490; (707) 459-5969

Neway, 150 Causeway Street, Boston, MA 02114; (617) 227-5117

Nexxus Products Co., P. O. Box 1274, Santa Barbara, CA 93116; (805) 968-6900

No Common Scents, King's Yard, Yellow Springs, OH 45387; (513) 767-4261

North Country, 7888 Country Road, #6, Maple Plain, MN 55359; (612) 479-3381

Nutri-Metics International, Inc., 3530 Pine Valley Drive, Sarasota, FL 34239; (813) 924-3251

Optikem International, Inc., 2172 South Jason Street, Denver, CO 80223; (303) 936-1137

Oriental Beauty Secrets (*see* G. T. International)

Orjene Natural Cosmetics, 5–43 48th Avenue, Long Island City, NY 11101; (718) 937-2666

Oxyfresh USA, Inc., East 10906 Marietta, P. O. Box 3723, Spokane, WA 99220; (509) 924-4999

Pagrovian Research (*see* Pro-Life Natural)

Panache (*see* Marie Lacoste Enterprises, Inc.)

Para Laboratories, Inc., 100 Rose Avenue, Hempstead, NY 11550; (516) 538-4600

Patricia Allison, 4470 Monahan Road, La Mesa, CA 92041; (619) 444-4879

Paul Penders (*see* D + P Products, Inc.)

Peelu Products, Ltd., 6224 Madison Court, Morton Grove, IL 60053; (312) 519-4496

Pets 'n' People, Inc., 5312 Ironwood, Rancho Palos Verdes, CA 90274; (213) 373-1559

Professional & Technical Services, Inc., 3331 Northeast Sandy Boulevard, Portland, OR 97232; (503) 231-7244

Pro-Life Natural, P. O. Box 13, Pacific Grove, CA 93950; (408) 373-7536

Puritan's Pride, 105 Orville Drive, Bohemia, NY 11716; (516) 567-9500

Queen Helene Beauty Products (*see* Para Laboratories)

Rachel Perry, Inc., 9111 Mason Avenue, Chatsworth, CA 91311; (818) 888-5881

Rainbow Research Corp., P. O. Box 153, Bohemia, NY 11716; (516) 589-5563

Reviva Labs, 705 Hopkins Road, Haddonfield, NJ 08033; (609) 428-3885

Scarborough & Company (*see* Crabtree & Evelyn, Ltd.)

Sebastian International, Inc., 6160 Variel Avenue, Woodland Hills, CA 91367; (818) 999-5112

Shahin Soap Co., P. O. Box 2413, 427 Van Dyke Avenue, Paterson, NJ 07509; (201) 790-4296

Shaklee U.S., Inc., Shaklee Terrace, 444 Market Street, San Francisco, CA 94111; (415) 954-3000

Shikai, P. O. Box 9637, Santa Rosa, CA 95405; (707) 584-0298

Sierra Dawn Products, 8687 Graton Road, Sebastopol, CA 95472; (707) 823-3920

Sirena Tropical Soap Co., P. O. Box 31673, Dallas, TX 75231; (214) 243-1991

The Soap Opera of Madison, WI, 319 State Street, Madison, WI 53703; (603) 251-4051

Sombra Cosmetics, Inc., 5600-G McLeod, NE, Albuquerque, NM 87109; (505) 888-0288

Sparkle (see A. J. Funk and Co.)

St. Ives Laboratories, Inc., 8944 Mason Avenue, Chatsworth, CA 91311; (818) 709-5500

Sunshine Fragrance Therapy, 1919 Burnside Avenue, Los Angeles, CA 90016; (213) 939-6400

Terra Nova, 650 University Avenue, Berkeley, CA 94710; (415) 841-0124

Tom's of Maine, Railroad Avenue, P. O. Box 710, Kennebunk, ME 04043; (207) 985-2944

Tri Hair Care Products (see Institute of Trichology)

Velvet Products Co., P. O. Box 5459, Beverly Hills, CA 90210; (213) 472-6431

Visage Beauté Cosmetics, Inc., P. O. Box 10928, Beverly Hills, CA 90213; (213) 273-9550

Vita Wave Products, 7131 Owensmouth Avenue, #94D, Canoga Park, CA 91303; (818) 886-3808

Viviane Woodard Skincare Cosmetics, 7712 Densmore Avenue, Van Nuys, CA 91406-1982; (818) 989-5818

Warm Earth Pottery & Cosmetics, 334 West 19th Street, Chico, CA 95928; (916) 895-0455

Weleda, Inc., 841 South Main Street, P. O. Box 769, Spring Valley, NY 10977; (914) 352-6145

Wysong Corporation, 1880 North Eastman, Midland, MI 48640; (517) 631-0009

Zia Cosmetics, 300 Brannan Street, Suite 601, San Francisco, CA 94107; (415) 543-7546

COMPANIES THAT DISTRIBUTE PRODUCTS NOT TESTED ON ANIMALS

The following companies distribute products that are not tested on animals:

ABEnterprises, P. O. Box 120220, Staten Island, NY 10312-0006; no telephone listed

Amberwood, Route 1, Box 206, Milner, GA 30257; (404) 358-2991

Arbonne International, Inc., P. O. Box 759, Lake Forest, CA 92630; (714) 770-2610

Baudelaire, Inc., Forest Road, Marlow, NH 03456; (603) 352-9234

Beauty Naturally, 57 Bosque Road, P. O. Box 426, Fairfax, CA 94930; (415) 459-2826

Bodywares, 2000 Pennsylvania Avenue NW, Washington, DC 20006; (202) 785-0716

Bonne Sante, 462 62nd Street, Brooklyn, NY 11220; (718) 492-3887

Carole's Cosmetics, 3081 Klondike Avenue, Costa Mesa, CA 92626; no telephone listed

A Clear Alternative, 8707 West Lane, Magnolia, TX 77355; (713) 356-7031

The Compassionate Consumer, Inc., P. O. Box 27, Jericho, NY 11753; (718) 445-4134

Cosmetic Technology, Inc., 4 Embarcadero Center 5100, San Francisco, CA 94111; (408) 761-2144

Erbe, 196 Prince Street, New York, NY 10012; (212) 966-1445

Everybody, Ltd., 1738 Pearl Street, Boulder, CO 80302; (303) 440-0188

Genesis, Inc., 67A Galli Drive, Novato, CA 94949; no telephone listed

Heart's Desire Mail-Order Co., 1307 Dwight Way, Berkeley, CA 94702; no telephone listed

Humane Street U.S.A., 467 Saratoga Avenue, Suite 300, San Jose, CA 95129; (408) 243-2530

Kim's Kruelty-Free Products, 41 Tallow Court, Quail Meadows, Woodlawn, MD 21207; (301) 597-8691

Kind Kare, Inc., 134 West University, Suite 125, Rochester, MI 48063; (313) 651-2032

Lion & Lamb Cruelty-Free Products, Inc., 29–28 41st Avenue, Long Island, NY 11101; (718) 361-5757

Milchin German Beauty Care Products, Biologische Kosmetik, 3714 Ridge Road, Nederland, CO 80466; (303) 444-0677

My Brother's Keeper, Inc., P. O. Box 1769, Richmond, IN 47375; (317) 962-5079

Nature Basics, 61 Main Street, Lancaster, NH 03584; (603) 788-4500

Panacea, P. O. Box 294, Columbia, PA 16512; no telephone listed

The Peaceable Kingdom, 1902 West 6th Street, Wilmington, DE 19805; (302) 429-8687

Shirley Price Aromatherapy (*see* Bonne Santé)

Spare the Animals, Inc., Cruelty-Free Products, P. O. Box 233, Tiverton, RI 02878; (401) 625-5963

Sunrise Lane Products, Inc., Dept. HS, 780 Greenwich Street, New York, NY 10014; no telephone listed

Vegan Street, P. O. Box 5525, Rockville, MD 20855; (301) 869-0086

Use Homemade Household Product Recipes

To be sure that your home is truly humane, you may make any of the household solutions in the following recipes. This list has been created by People for the Ethical Treatment of Animals (PETA).

CLEANSERS

CAMP COOKWARE

Wash with a baking soda solution or shake baking soda on a damp sponge to remove cooked-on food or grease.

WINE/COFFEE STAINS

Blot the fresh spill with a cloth soaked with club soda.

COOKING UTENSILS
Let pots and pans soak in a baking soda solution before washing.

COPPER CLEANER
Use a paste of lemon juice, salt, and flour; or rub vinegar and salt into the copper.

FURNITURE POLISH
Mix three parts olive oil and one part vinegar, or one part lemon juice and two parts olive oil. Use a soft cloth.

GENERAL CLEANER
Mix baking soda with a small amount of water.

GLASS CLEANER
Use white vinegar or rubbing alcohol and water.

HEADLIGHT, MIRROR, WINDSHIELD CLEANER
Wipe with a damp cloth or sponge sprinkled with baking soda. Rinse with water and dry with a soft towel.

HOUSEHOLD CLEANER
Use three tablespoons baking soda mixed into one quart warm water.

LINOLEUM FLOOR CLEANER
Use one cup of white vinegar mixed with two gallons of water to wash, club soda to polish.

MICROWAVE OVENS
Clean and deodorize the insides of the oven and around the door seal with a baking soda solution. For stubborn odors, leave an open box of baking soda inside, but be sure to remove it before each use of the oven.

MILDEW REMOVER
Use lemon juice or white vinegar and salt.

OIL AND GREASE ON DRIVEWAY

Remove by sprinkling the area with kitty litter, allowing it to absorb. Then remove it with a shovel or broom.

OIL STAIN REMOVER

Rub white chalk into the stain before laundering.

MISCELLANEOUS

AIR FRESHENER

Leave an opened box of baking soda in the room or add cloves and cinnamon to boiling water and simmer. Scent the house with fresh flowers or herbs; or open windows (in the winter, for about fifteen minutes every morning).

DRAIN OPENER

Prevent clogging by using a drain strainer or by flushing a drain weekly with boiling water. If clogged, pour one-half cup baking soda, then one-half cup vinegar, down the drain.

FERTILIZER

Use compost.

ODOR REMOVER

On carpet or furniture (from spills or accidents), blot the fresh stain with a cloth soaked with cider vinegar.

WATER SOFTENER

Use one-quarter cup vinegar in the final rinse.

NOTE

Some vinegar may be filtered through gelatin, which comes from animal by-products. You may want to use unfiltered vinegar.

Commercially produced cruelty-free household products are also available. Write to PETA for a free list of compassionate companies.

Use Homemade Cosmetic and Facial Recipes

There is not an animal on the earth, nor a flying creature on two
wings, but they are people like unto you.

—The Koran

Instead of using products that exploit animals and
harm the environment, pamper yourself with some
of our skin and beauty recipes, listed here.

FACIALS

CORNMEAL RUB

If you have dry skin, apply almond oil first. If
skin is oily, simply moisten with water. Rub corn-
meal over face in small circles and stop when face
feels warm and flushed. Rince face with warm
water.

JUICE RUB

When skin is irritated and dry from too much
sun or heat, rub with juices from strawberry,
peach, or cucumber at night.

AVOCADO CLEANSER

Massage mashed avocado into skin for several minutes. This cleanses and conditions dry skin.

BUTTERMILK LOTION

This is good for all skin types. Apply directly to cleanse and soften.

BATHS

LEMON BATH

For oily skin—add one cupful of freshly squeezed lemon juice to your bath.

BAKING SODA BATH

For dry, irritated skin—add one-half cup baking soda to the bath.

BODY POWDER

CORNSTARCH

This is good for baby's diaper rash, adult sweat rash, or prickly heat.

SKIN CARE

DRY-SKIN LOTION

Pierce and squeeze out a dozen each of Vitamin E and A capsules into a bottle, add a few drops of your favorite fragrance, shake well, and apply on skin as needed.

OILY-SKIN LOTION

Mix equal proportions of warm water and freshly squeezed and strained lime juice to cleanse and refresh skin.

SUN LOTIONS

MOISTURIZER

Simply rub a freshly peeled cucumber over dry facial and other skin areas. Sesame oil stays on even when you go into the water. It keeps skin moist and prevents burning. For sunburn, apply vinegar or yogurt or a paste of baking soda.

TOOTHPASTE

Mix equal parts of salt and baking soda. Add a few drops of wintergreen or peppermint oil for flavor. (This is only to be used by adults. Baking soda does not contain fluoride, which is important for children's teeth.)

For other recipes, including shampoos and hair conditioners, see Donna Lawson's *Mother Nature's Beauty Cupboard*. New York, Bantam Books; 1974.

Buy Toys Made By Companies That Don't Test Their Products on Animals

One of the objectives of education from nursery school onwards must be to give children a balanced sensitivity to life.
—Canadian Senate Committee on Health, Welfare and Science

Though it is not commonly known, some toy companies exploit animals as cruelly as do cosmetics and household-products firms. For instance, some manufacturers—or the labs they contract—test projectile toys by shooting them into rabbits' eyes. Toy materials such as dyes, paints, and stuffing have been toxicity-tested with the LD-50 and other tests.

For your guidance, we are including a list of toy companies that do test on animals, and a list of those that do not. The list was produced from a survey conducted by People for the Ethical Treatment of Animals.

TOY COMPANIES THAT DO TEST ON ANIMALS

The following companies have stated that they *DO* test their toys on animals.*

Fisher-Price, 636 Girard Avenue, East Aurora, NY 14052-1885
LJN Toys Ltd., 200 5th Avenue, New York, NY 10010
Shelcore Inc., 3474 South Clinton Avenue, South Plainfield, NJ 07080
Spearhead Industries Inc., 9971 Valley View Road, Minneapolis, MN 55344

TOY COMPANIES THAT DO NOT TEST ON ANIMALS

The following companies have signed a statement of assurance that they *do not* test their toys on animals.*

American Plastic Toys, 799 Ladd Road, Walled Lake, MI 48088
A.R.C. Division of Athol Industries, P. O. Box 246, Athol, ME 01331
Aristoplay, P. O. Box 7028, Ann Arbor, MI 48107
Artwood, P. O. Box 207, Woodland, GA 31836
Axtell Expressions, 272 Dalton Street, Ventura, CA 93003
Bigtoys, 2601 South Hood Street, Tacoma, WA 98409
B. J. Toy Co. Inc., 504 Applegate Avenue, P. O. Box 58, Pen Argyle, PA 18072
Bolink R/C Cars Inc., 420 Hosea Road, Lawrenceville, GA 30245
Bremen Corp., P. O. Box 70, Bremen, IN 46506
Buddy L. Toys, 200 Fifth Avenue, New York, NY 10010
Burnham Associates Inc., 26 Dearborn Street, Salem, MA 01970
Carousel Industries, 6340 Oakton Street, Morton Grove, IL 60053
The Cavalier Group, 7510 Hornwood, Houston, TX 77036
Changing Scenes, P. O. Box 1058, Cardiff, CA 92007
Choteau Activities Inc., P. O. Box 799, Choteau, MT 59422
Classic Balloon Corp., 15173 Business Avenue, Dallas, TX 75234
Classic Toy Co., 2320 Superior Ave., Cleveland, OH 44144
Colorforms, 133 Williams Drive, Ramsey, NJ 07466
Creative Playthings Ltd., 33 Loring Drive, Framingham, MA 01701
Daisy Manufacturing Co., Box 220, Rogers, AR 72757

---
*A company's exclusion from this list does not necessarily mean that it does not use animals. There are many companies that we have not yet heard from, as well as some that refuse to answer. When in doubt, contact us.

D.C.S. Inc., 517 Otteray Drive, High Point, NC 27262

Developmental Playcraft Inc., 800 MacArthur Boulevard, Springfield, IL 62702

Diener Industries Inc., 20257 Prairie Street, Chatsworth, CA 91313-4057

Fantasy Toys Inc., P. O. Box 1282, Fair Oaks, CA 95628

Floquil-Poly S Color Corp., Route 30 North, Amsterdam, NY 12010

The Frenry Company, 14480 62nd Street North, Clearwater, FL 34620

Frivals 'N Friends, P. O. Box 801101, Dallas, TX 75380

Game Inventors of America, 4809 W. Moreland, Dallas, TX 75237

Gamers Guild Mfg., P. O. Box 660, Quanah, TX 79252

Gamescience, 1512 30th Avenue, Gulfport, MS 39501

Greenleaf Products, Box 388, 58 North Main Street, Honeoye Falls, NY 14472

Greenwood Intl. of America Inc., 8910 Purdeu Road, Indianapolis, IN 46268

Hasbro Inc., 1027 Newport Avenue, Pawtucket, RI 02862-1059

Hip Yik International, 1045 North 7th Street, San Jose, CA 95112

Importoys Inc., P. O. Box 92455, Los Angeles, CA 90009

James Industries Inc., P. O. Box 407, Hollidaysburg, PA 16648

Jesmar of Miami, 3012 Northwest 79th Avenue, Miami, FL 33122

Kenner Products, 1014 Vine Street, Cincinnati, OH 45202

Kilgore Corp., Bradford Road, Toone, TN 38381-0099

Lee Alum. Foundry and Mfg. Co., New Albin, Iowa 52601

Lego Systems Inc., 555 Taylor Road, Enfield, CT 06082

The Little Tikes Co., 2180 Barlow Road, Hudson, OH 44236

Logical Nonsense Inc., P. O. Box 22, Cambridge, MA 02238

Lovee Doll & Toy Co., 303 Stanley Avenue, Brooklyn, NY 11207

Manatee Toy Co. Inc., 131 Beach Lane, Crystal Lane, FL 32629

Mapes Industries Inc., 6 Grace Avenue, Great Neck, NY 11021

Marksman Products, 5622 Engineer Drive, Huntington Beach, CA 92649

Marlon Creations Inc., 35-01 36 Avenue, Long Island City, NY 11106

Mary Meyer Corp., Townshend, VT 05353

Mattel Inc., 5150 Rosecrans Avenue, Hawthorne, CA 90250-6692

Molor Products Co., 643 Blackhawk Drive, Westmont, IL 60559

Nashco Products Inc., 1015 Main Street, Scranton, PA 18504

The National Latex Products Co., 246 East 4th Street, Ashland, OH 44805

North American Bear Co. Inc., 401 North Wabash River, Chicago, IL 60611

Olmec, 7 West 22nd Street, New York, NY 10010

The Paper Soldier, 8 McIntosh Lane, Clifton, NY 12065

Parma International Inc., 13927 Progress Parkway, North Royalton, OH 44133

Parris Mfg. Co., Box 338, Savannah, TN 38372

Pastime Industries Inc., 21 Hall Street, Brooklyn, NY 11205

Peck-Polymers, P. O. Box 2498, La Mesa, CA 92044

Personal Creations, 2710 North Cotner, Lincoln, NE 68504

Pioneer Balloon Co., 555 North Woodlawn Avenue, Wichita, KS 67208

Play Jour Inc., 200 5th Avenue, New York, NY 10010

The Play Mill, RFD 3, Box 89, Dover-Foxcroft, ME 04426

Playmobil USA Inc., 100 Newfield Avenue, Edison, NJ 08837

Playspaces International Inc., 31-D Union Avenue, Sudbury, MA 01776

Pleasant Co., 8400 Fairway Place, P. O. Box 998, Middleton, WI 53562-0998

Precision Scale Co., P. O. Box 1262, Woodland, CA 95695-1262

PTN Industries, Ford Ave., P. O. Box 370, Milltown, NJ 08850

Ramagon Toys Inc., 618 Northwest Glisan Street, Suite 205, Portland, OR 97209

Ramona Plush Toy Corp., 6100 Wilson Road, Kansas City, MO 64123-1943

Ray Plastic Inc., Winchendon Springs, MA 01477

Real Good Toys Inc., P. O. Box 706, Montpelier, VT 05602

R. E. Greenspan Co. Inc., 10073 Sandmeyer Lane, Philadelphia, PA 19116

Rose Art Industries Inc., 53 La France Avenue, Bloomfield, NJ 07003

Royal House of Dolls, 65 Hope Street, Brooklyn, NY 11211

Sega of America, 573 Forbes Boulevard, San Francisco, CA 94080

Solargraphics, P. O. Box 7091, Berkeley, CA 94707

Sonic-Tronics Inc., 7865 Mill Road, Elkins Park, PA 19117

Sports Products Corp., 4701 Manufacturing Road, Cleveland, OH 44133

St. Louis Crafts Inc., 44 Kirkham Industrial Court, St. Louis, MO 63119

Steven Mfg. Co., 224 East 4th Street, P. O. Box 275, Hermann, MO 65041

Stuhr Enterprises, 51 4th Avenue, Moline, IL 61265

Superior Toy and Novelty Corp., 1117 West 8th Street, Kansas City, MO 64101

Today's Kids, Highway 10 East, Booneville, AR 72927

The Toy Works Inc., P. O. Box 48, Middle Falls, NY 12848

Toymex S.A., 231 Pulin Avenue, Calexico, CA 92231

Toys By Daphne Inc., 301 West Marshall Avenue, Phoenix, AZ 85013

Tyco Industries Inc., 540 Glen Avenue, Moorestown, NJ 08057
Underground Toys and Gifts, 1616½ W. 11th, Eugene, OR 97402
Unique Industries Inc., 2400 South Weccacoe Avenue, Philadelphia, PA 19148
Walnut Hollow Farm Inc., Route 2, Dodgeville, WI 53533
Weaver's Bottom Craft Studio, Berea, KY 40403
Worlds of Wonder Inc., 4209 Technology Drive, Fremont, CA 94538
Yaley Enterprises, P. O. Box 2225, San Francisco, CA 94080
Yankee Doodle Woodworkers, 500 Pershing Avenue, P. O. Box 600, Scituate, MA 02066

---

*A company's exclusion from this list does not necessarily mean that it tests on animals. There are many companies we have not yet heard from, as well as some that refuse to answer.

Write to Corporations Violating Your Animal Ethic

It should not be believed that all beings exist for the sake of the existence of man. On the contrary, all the other beings too have been intended for their own sakes and not for the sake of anything else.

—Maimonides

Write to companies that manufacture household products and cosmetics and demand that they find non-animal methods to test for irritancy. Write to companies that have declared a moratorium on such tests and encourage them to make the move permanent. Write to toy manufacturers and demand that they stop testing their toys on animals. Tell them that you will boycott their products—and urge your friends to do the same—unless they adopt a more humane approach. Please use the addresses we have supplied.

For the latest list of companies to be boycotted because of cruelty to animals and other abuses, including risks to the environment, employees, and consumers, subscribe to *Boycott News,* published by Co-op America, 2100 M Street NW, Suite 310, Washington, DC 20036.

V
THE DISCRIMINATING DRESSER

Don't Wear Fur

Killing an animal to make a coat is a sin. It wasn't meant to be, and we have no right to do it. A woman gains status when she refuses to see anything killed to be put on her back. Then she's truly beautiful.

—Doris Day

Wear no wild-animal furs, even if the particular animal is not named on the endangered-species list. These animals are inhumanely caught and killed, and their use for personal decoration alone is unacceptable.

According to the Humane Society of the United States, about three-quarters of all pelts produced in the U.S. come from wild animals, including foxes, coyotes, raccoons, bobcats, beavers, muskrats, badgers, otters, opossums, and minks. (The fur industry gives these pelts a low profile by selling them abroad. The U.S., it turns out, is the world's largest exporter of pelts, just about all of them from trapped animals.)

Most of the 22 million animals trapped for their fur in the U.S. each year are caught with what is known as the "leghold trap"—a torturous device that often crushes the animal's limb, keeping the animal trapped for up to two weeks until the trapper returns. Other traps include the neck snare, which slowly strangles victims over a period of hours or days, and the whole-body trap, which induces prolonged and excruciating pain.

Many trapped creatures die from dehydration, starvation, or exhaustion in their traps. Others are killed by predators. If trappers find their quarry alive, they may break their necks (by hand or with mechanical devices), beat them to death with a blunt instrument, slam them against trees or rocks, or suffocate or drown them.

What's more, this cruelty is actually subsidized by the U.S. government! For instance, the government maintains state trapping authorities, which then collect license fees. And the Animal Damage Control branch of the U.S. Department of Agriculture (USDA) actually controls 51,000 traps. The USDA also spends millions of dollars to promote fur sales overseas.

Finally, be aware of the plight of millions of "trash animals"—those accidentally caught in traps and then summarily discarded. These "trash animals" include pets such as cats and dogs, as well as deer, skunk, and even endangered species like the grizzly bear and the bald eagle.

Many people believe that while wild-animal furs are verboten, it's okay to wear fur that comes from animals raised on a "ranch." Nothing could be further from the truth. The term "ranch" is a misnomer; fur ranching is every bit as cruel as fur trapping. Here's why: Minks, rabbits, foxes, and beavers raised on ranches are not domesticated. It would take thousands of years to truly domesticate such creatures, after all, not just a few generations.

These animals are every bit as wild as those actually living in the wilderness. Imagine how these wild creatures must feel when, instead of traversing a range of several square miles, they find themselves trapped from birth in wire-mesh cages so tiny that they can barely turn around. Beset by unbearable claustrophobia and terror, these animals go into a frenzy with each intruder and every new sound. In fact, the tension they feel results in endless pacing, self-mutilation, and high rates of cannibalism in mother/infant groups, especially among foxes.

If life is unpleasant for these animals, so is death. Many have their necks broken, sometimes with mechanical devices; others are electrocuted; and yet others are gassed with carbon monoxide or carbon dioxide. Death by gas is particularly painful—and not always effective. Many animals don't actually die, and then they find themselves revived while being skinned!

Do not contribute to this flagrant, horrific abuse. Cloth coats, wool sweaters, and Kapok-filled jackets and parkas will keep you just as warm as fur.

You can also fight against the use of fur by expressing your outrage to others. Tell your friends and family the truth about their fur coats and fur-lined gloves. You might also express yourself through a letter to the Op-Ed page of your local paper and any magazine that carries ads for fur coats and accessories.

20

Do Not Buy Garments or Accessories Made with Seal Pelts

Modern man no longer regards Nature as being in any sense divine and feels perfectly free to behave toward her as an overweening conqueror and tyrant.

—Aldous Huxley

Although you should not wear fur from any animal, the plight of seal pups killed for their pelts is especially grave. Each year, thousands of fur seals are clubbed to death in Canada and the U.S. Often, baby seals, the most sought after, are skinned alive, their carcasses left with their distraught mothers.

In Canada, harp seals are approached on the ice by sealers who club a pup, slit its main arteries, and peel off the pelt in less than two minutes. The pelts are usually shipped away to Norway for processing, then sold in Europe and Canada in the form of fur collars and cuffs, glove linings, key chains, and stuffed-toy seals.

Though the Canadian government claims that this hunt is necessary to control seal overpopulation, most scientists don't agree. They say the current kill quotas threaten the species' very existence.

The U.S. government, meanwhile, sponsors an annual hunt for the North Pacific fur seal on Alaska's Pribilof Islands. (Similar kills take place on Cammander and Robben islands in the Soviet Union, as well.) There, the seals are rounded up and clubbed to death.

Pelts are processed by a single U.S. company—the Fouke Fur Company of South Carolina—and made into women's full-length fur coats and other garments. Aleut natives conduct the kill, from which virtually their only source of income is provided.

The slaughter must stop; at the current rate of killing, the seal population is declining by 8 to 10 percent a year. The Aleuts can either diversify their economy and develop other industries now, or be forced to do so in the near future—when the fur seals have become extinct.

ANIMALS AT RISK

Species of animals killed legally and illegally for fur and skin include:

Alpaca	Cat, Manul	Fisher
Antelope	Cat, Margay	Fitch
Badger	Cat, Spotted	Fox
Bassarisk	Cat, Wild	Fox, Arctic
Bear, Black	Cheetah	Fox, Black
Bear, Brown	Chinchilla	Fox, Blue
Bear, Polar	Chipmunk	Fox, Cross
Beaver	Civet	Fox, Grey
Buffalo	Cougar	Fox, Kit
Burunduk	Coyote	Fox, Platinum
Calf	Desman	Fox, Red
Cat, Caracal	Dog	Fox, Silver
Cat, Domestic	Ermine	Fox, White
Cat, Lynx	Ferret	Genet

Goat
Guanaco or its young, the
    guanaquito
Hamster
Hare
Jackal
Jackal, Cape
Jaguar
Jaguarondi
Kangaroo
Kangaroo-rat
Kid
Kinkajou
Koala
Kolinsky
Lamb
Leopard
Llama
Lynx
Marmot
Marten, American
Marten, Baum
Marten, Japanese
Marten, Stone
Mink
Mole
Monkey
Muskrat
Nutria
Ocelot
Opossum
Opossum, Ring-tail
Opossum, South American
Opossum, Water
Otter
Otter, Sea
Pahmi
Panda
Peschanik
Pony

Rabbit
Raccoon
Raccoon, Asiatic
Raccoon, Mexican
Reindeer
Sable
Sable, American
Sable, Russian
Seal, Fur
Seal, Barkal
Seal, Bearded
Seal, Caspisian
Seal, Hair
Seal, Harbor
Seal, Harp
Seal, Hooded
Seal, Largha
Seal, Northern Fur
Seal, Ribbon
Seal, Ringed
Seal, Rock
Seal, South African Fur
Seal, South American Fur
Sheep
Skunk
Skunk, Spotted
Squirrel
Squirrel, Flying
Suslik
Vicuna
Viscacha
Wallaby
Weasel
Weasel, Chinese
Weasel, Japanese
Weasel, Manchurian
Wolf
Wolverine
Wombat
Woodchuck

Wear Animal-Friendly Fabrics

Until he extends the circle of his compassion to all living things, man will not himself find peace.

—Albert Schweitzer

Some conscientious humanitarians go so far as to eschew wearing anything made of animal origin. These people will not wear silk, because the fabric comes from the silkworm pupae that are boiled alive. Nor will they wear wool, often derived from sheep and angora goats raised in confinement sheds or produced by ranchers who overgraze the land and indiscriminately poison and trap predators.

But you need not boycott all animal fabrics. For instance, you *can* find humane and ecologically friendly wool producers and products, especially from the rural cottage industries of New England. The rule of thumb, however, is to own few woolens—buy wool infrequently, and remember to repair, not discard, the wool items that you have.

There are certain synthetics to beware of, as well. Nylon and polyester materials don't biodegrade.

And remember, use a sparing approach with cotton and flax—production generally entails significant use of pesticides.

In general, keep in mind that the smaller your wardrobe, the less energy you consume: Cotton and wool are more economical than synthetic materials such as polyester. Kapok and other synthetic fibers are more humane insulators of parkas than duck and goose down.

22

Use Leather Alternatives

If you have men who will exclude any of God's creatures from the shelter of compassion and pity, you will have men who will deal likewise with their fellow men.

—Francis of Assisi

Some people reason that leather is a by-product of the meat industry, not to be wasted. Others refuse to purchase even the smallest leather accessory, from belts and jackets to pocketbooks and shoes. (The smell makes some folks sick, and the black-leather bomber jacket certainly links meat with machismo.)

The true animal activist will avoid leather at all costs, especially since leather alternatives are attractive and easy to find. Cotton-canvas bags and shoes are practical and sturdy, as are cloth coats, jackets, and belts. Vinyl is a viable alternative, as well.

One note: Be wary of plastic alternatives, since plastics do not biodegrade.

VI
FEROCIOUS
FRIVOLITIES

Do Not Buy Ivory

Man, do not pride yourself on your superiority to animals: they are without sin, and you, with your greatness, defile the earth by your appearance on it, and leave the traces of your foulness after you.
— Fyodor Mikhailovich Dostoyevsky

As you no doubt know, ivory used to make jewelry, figurines, and piano keys comes largely from the tusk of the African elephant. (Some comes from the walrus, as well.) With 80,000 elephants slain each year, their plight has now become critical. Each day, entire herds are poisoned or wiped out with machine guns. Some poachers even hack off the faces of living animals to acquire the ivory that appears in stores around the world. At the current rate of slaughter, the experts say, the African elephant will become extinct in five to ten years.

To help the African elephant, we suggest that you buy no ivory. Tell your friends to do the same. Do not shop anywhere that ivory is sold. Also tell stores, mail-order houses, and advertisers that you will not patronize them or buy their products as long as they sell or promote ivory.

You can also write to the U.S. Department of the Interior, 18th and C Streets NW, Washington DC 20240. Explain in your letter that you would like to see the African elephant declared an endangered species. When the elephant receives endangered-species status, commercial trade in ivory will be illegal.

Finally, write to your congressional representative and two senators, asking them to support endangered-species status for the African elephant. You can reach your representative at the U.S. House of Representatives, Washington DC 20515. You can reach both your state senators at the U.S. Senate, Washington DC 20510.

24

Reject Animal Art

Until we stop harming all other living beings, we are still savages.
—Thomas Edison

Do not buy art and jewelry based on animal exploitation. Materials to avoid include ivory, of course, but also tortoiseshell, bird feathers, butterflies, shells obtained from sea creatures still alive, animal skins, animal teeth, and animal claws and bones. We also suggest that you refuse to buy coral jewelry or souvenirs, since living coral reefs are being decimated by overharvesting and pollution.

Finally, if you are going abroad, upon your return you may be stopped by U.S. Customs agents if you carry any products made from endangered species. These products will be confiscated. Remember, foreign stores will not *tell* you that their products have been made from these species. In some instances, a retailer may tell you that the product (an alligator handbag, say, or a deer-skin jacket) is derived from ranch-raised, captive animals, implying that the species is not endangered.

But that does not make the product more acceptable to the humane consumer, since the animals were killed for trivial gratuitous purposes, and countless species not yet officially listed as endangered are indeed in danger of extinction. So the best advice is this: Do not buy *any* animal product at home or abroad.

Protest Rodeos

It may well be that man's attitude to the animal world spills over into his attitude to his own fellows. The exploitation of the one springs from the same temper of mind that exploits the other.
—Rev. Edward Carpenter

Rodeo animals are used over and over again in practice and training sessions and are forced to perform in actual events an average of every two and a half days. This exhausting and painful regimen regularly results in bruises caused by rearing while trapped in a chute; abrasion from being raked by the rider's spurs; muscle or tendon injuries caused by bucking around the arena; and the terror of being shocked by electric prods.

In the horrific event of calf-roping, a baby calf forced to run from the chute may be moving as fast as twenty-seven miles an hour when the lasso tightens around its neck. The cowboy's goal: to fling the calf to the ground and tie together three of its legs in ten seconds or less. Obviously, injuries including a bruised larynx, a broken neck, or internal hemorrhaging abound.

Steer-roping, in which the animal must be thrown to the ground by a rope, is appalling, as well. The steer's horns may be broken and, not infrequently, one or more limbs may be injured in the process.

Rodeos sponsored by the Professional Rodeo Cowboy's Association (PRCA), while still cruel, do have some rules that render the events somewhat less violent. These constitute only 30 percent of all rodeos, however; the other 70 percent, sponsored mostly by schools, community groups, and lodges, are run by the philosophy of "anything goes." Usually conducted without an attending veterinarian or guidelines as to how animals should be treated, these events are a good target for local citizens willing to campaign against rodeos.

We urge you to refuse to attend any rodeo for entertainment, though you may want to attend one to familiarize yourself with the ways in which animals are mistreated. Any rodeo event broadcast on television is worth a letter of complaint to the station. (See network addresses, page 119.) We also suggest that you campaign against rodeos in your area. If your local rodeo is not sanctioned by the PRCA, your chance of convincing local officials to cancel the event may be particularly good.

26

Boycott Animal Acts

The original meaning of dominion for the book of *Genesis* comes from the Hebrew root verb *Yorade*. This literally means to go down, to have sympathy for and communion with fellow creatures. It is an injunction to care for creation with respect and compassion.
—Rabbi Harold White

Do not attend the circus, aquarium shows, or any other shows at which animals are forced to perform tricks.

We believe that any use of animals for mere entertainment is inherently cruel. In the circus, wild animals are deprived of their natural environment and, in essence, imprisoned for life. These animals are generally kept isolated in tiny cages as the circus travels from town to town. Larger animals like elephants are chained together and attached to a trailer or building so that they can barely move. These animals often exercise only when rehearsing and performing their acts, under the dominion of man.

The fate of chimpanzees, orangutans, and other circus primates may be particularly grave. Trainers generally treat these animals abusively, even beating them repeatedly to establish and maintain dominance over them. Some even control these creatures with remote-control electric shock prods, attached to the animal's body. In some cases the shock is so severe that the animal convulses and vomits.

Forcing circus, zoo, and aquarium animals to perform tricks is demeaning. The animals suppress their true nature and turn into obedient puppets. Such animal performances are anti-educational, since children get a wholly erroneous view of the animals' true nature, behavior, and intelligence. In fact, we believe that even under the best conditions, the circus is inhumane.

Even if a trainer or animal handler loves animals, as soon as these animals begin to perform, what emerges is not love, but rather domination. Domination—the need to have power and control over other beings—comes not from love but from fear. The more you empathize with animals forced to perform, the less you will be entertained and the more you will be repulsed.

Also, keep in mind that there are many alternatives to the circus, from soccer, baseball, and football for the observer, to nature photography, hiking, and camping for those who like participating in activities themselves.

Ride Roadside Zoos Out of Town

Butterfly, butterfly, why come you here?
   This is no bower for you;
Go sip the honey-drop sweet and clear,
   Or bathe in the morning dew.

This is the place to think of heaven,
   This is the place to pray;
You have no sins to be forgiven—
   Butterfly—go away.
                              —William Cowper

The inmates are bears and lions, parrots and chimpanzees. They spend their lives behind bars, often alone, in tiny, dilapidated cells with no room to exercise, no bedding, and no shelter from the elements. Often, their keepers engineer these lives of unbearable misery and boredom to attract tourists, who may then also patronize nearby gas stations, stores, and motels.

In a recent investigation of these facilities in Florida, Jeanne Roush, former director of captive wildlife protection for the Humane Society of the United States, uncovered what she called a "skid row" for animals. Her inspection report details a litany of abuses: disrepair, cage floors encrusted with feces and vomit, rotted wooden sleeping shelves, rusted water pans, scum in drinking water, foul odors, swarms of flies, and on and on.

In some instances, roadside zoo keepers actually house nocturnal animals in scorching sunlight, depriving them of every natural means to seek shelter or cool off. Animals that naturally burrow have nowhere to burrow; those that swim are deprived of adequate water; and those that climb live without trees or even a mound of elevated dirt. Imagine a bobcat, which would normally travel five miles a day, spending its entire life in a cage the length and width of a mattress. Imagine a chimpanzee, a creature dependent on social contact, passing twenty years in solitary confinement in a dirty concrete cell. Envision a lion, honed through millions of years of evolution to explore the environment and develop bonds, left alone in a tiny cage for life with no diversion except its own feces.

To end abuses in the thousands of roadside zoos across the United States, you must refuse to patronize them. Be sure to tell your friends about roadside zoos; explain that if they patronize these houses of horror, they will be drastically increasing the suffering that animals are forced to endure. If there is a roadside zoo in your town, we suggest you check the place out; then write a letter to the editor of your local newspaper discussing the facility and explaining why it must be closed.

Since some of the worst abuses occur in the state of Florida, we urge you to write to the Florida Division of Tourism to express your outrage. Explain that these animal torture chambers make Florida an unattractive place for your next trip. Address your letters to: Mr. Dean Gaiser, Director,

Division of Tourism, 510-C Collins Building, Tallahassee, FL 32301.

MODERN ZOOS: AGENDA FOR THE 21ST CENTURY

Today, the best modern zoos claim to be advanced in conservation and in research into wildlife diseases, surgery, and reproduction. At places like the Bronx Zoo and the San Diego Zoo, many animals live in habitats which, to some degree, simulate their natural environments. These zoos, zoo directors claim, educate the public about the intricacies of animal life.

But it is important, even in light of these improvements, that we ask ourselves whether these zoos are doing an adequate job. After all, even in the best of zoos the animals are captives; even in the most humane of these facilities, creatures inhabit mere facsimiles of their natural environments, and, with their wild natures compromised, they lead unnaturally confined, sanitized lives.

There are those, of course, who claim that modern zoos are needed because they save species from extinction by keeping them in captivity. But we believe that if there is no further place now or in the future for these animals in the wild, it may be best to let them become extinct. Life in captivity can never fulfill any species, or any individual animal. An animal, after all, *is* its environment; without the environment that spawned it, the creature is incomplete.

The best zoos, of course, do have semi-natural environments, from mini-swamps to artificial rivers to climatrons. But toward what end? These facsimiles don't conserve these natural environments, they just serve to exhibit them. And even if such artificial environments can enhance the overall reproductivity of an individual species, the offspring of these animals will have nowhere to go—except to another zoo.

Ultimately, we believe, the new and improved zoo should strive to educate the public about the lives of animals in the wild today. Are we justified in keeping animals captive in zoos if films and documentaries actually do a better job of portraying the animals' lives?

We believe that in order to justify its existence, the modern zoo must begin to educate visitors about the true plight of all sorts of animals worldwide. For instance, the zoo does not show, as a film might, the effect that chemical pollution or radiation might have on the polar bear. Nor does it show fish from the Great Lakes exploding and eroding from cancer, even though these fish are plentiful.

Given the needs of animals around the world, the modern zoo must do more to provide visitors with appropriate compassion for species living in the wild. To be truly justified, zoos must inform—and even shock—the public into concern and political action on behalf of the animals represented within. And every zoo worth its salt should be involved in programs to protect endangered species in the wild by helping to preserve natural habitats at home and abroad.

28

Speak Out Against Animal "Sports"

We can find no difference between humans and animals that is morally relevant.

—Prof. Bernard Rollin

Avoid any "sport" that seems to abuse animals, from greased-pig catching to bullfights. Be alert for "sports" in your community such as prairie-dog shoots and rattlesnake roundups that serve no real environmental purpose. Numerous so-called sports use animals as erstwhile athletes, in the process imprisoning them, terrifying them, and subjecting them to painful injury and death. The "athletic events" to look out for—and avoid—include:

BULLFIGHTS

In Spain, Portugal, and Mexico, the bullfight continues to be a popular spectator sport; matadors, who slay the bulls, are often national heroes. But there's nothing brave about killing a bull. The animal is tormented, tortured, and weakened by having its neck and shoulder muscles speared and lanced repeatedly before the matador even enters the bull ring. Boycott bullfights if you go to these countries for business or pleasure. A letter of protest to the ministers of tourism of these countries and to their ambassadors in Washington, D.C., would also be worthwhile. Tell these officials that you won't vacation in their countries or buy any of their imported products until they put an end to bullfights.

PULLING CONTESTS

Horse bullock or pony-pulling contests are usually conducted by harnessing two animals to a heavy load and, following each round, adding several hundred additional pounds. Popular at fairs across the nation, especially in New England and the Midwest, pulling contests often involve brutal training regimens. Cattle prods, boards, clubs, whips, and even electrical currents from tractor batteries are all used to teach these animals to lunge forward with enough force to break a load free. Animals involved in pulling contests also suffer heat stress and overexertion; they are frequently drugged to reduce the pain of strained muscles and deprived of water so that they can qualify for lighter weight classes.

GREASED-PIG CONTESTS

Greased pigs in these events deal with enormous stress. Children chase them, teen-agers pounce on them, and handlers literally kick them to force them back into the arena. If sponsors were aware of the cruelty, they would probably be far more reluctant to schedule these events.

TURKEY DROPS

In this bizarre and terrifying event, turkeys are tossed to town residents from building roofs or small aircraft.

DONKEY BASKETBALL

People play an entire game of basketball astride donkeys' backs. As the game heats up, the animals are often kicked, punched, and shoved.

DOGFIGHTING

Dogfighting is a brutal sport in which dogs are trained to fight to the death while crowds of bettors cheer them on. Though this activity is illegal, dogfighting rings exist throughout the United States. If you become aware of dogfighting or dogfighting rings in your area, please contact legal authorities.

HORSE RACING

As conducted in the U.S., horse racing benefits horse owners, trainers, track veterinarians, and racetrack operators. As far as the horses are concerned, however, the abuses they suffer are legion. Animals being "urged" to run faster are often kicked, whipped, and drugged. Most horses begin their racing career at two years of age, before their musculoskeletal system is developed enough to withstand the rigors of racing—of course, needless injuries result. Many owners force their horses to race far too often; others give them pain-killing drugs, enabling them to run despite injuries. Racehorses are also often forced to run in extreme heat and cold, and on especially hard tracks, increasing race times—and injuries.

TENNESSEE-WALKING-HORSE RACES

These races may seem humane, but there's much cruelty in this business, too. In the process of training these horses to trot with their feet high in the air, weights are attached to their front feet. Caustic material is put just above the hoof, which may be drilled so that a pebble or piece of glass can be rammed inside. As a result, the animal develops the desired, high-stepping gait, lifting its feet ever higher in response to the pain.

DOG RACING

In the sport of dog racing, the abuse is twofold—the racing dogs suffer, and so do other animals used as bait to help them train. First of all, most of the greyhounds raised for racing each year do not exhibit enough speed to be successful; more than 50 percent of the greyhounds are thus killed before they even get to the track. Even dogs that have raced successfully are killed once they stop winning races, usually at the age of four. About 30,000 greyhounds are put to death or used in biomedical research each year. Others are adopted into homes and make excellent family companions. To adopt one, contact Greyhound Pets of America, Ms. Millie Merritt, 750 Willard St., Quincy, Mass., 02169.

COCKFIGHTING

In an organized cockfight, two specially bred roosters—equipped with incredibly sharp steel gaffs—are placed together in a pit. The animals then fight, usually to the death. Most fights in what is known as the "main pit" last up to fifteen minutes; injured animals are then placed in a "drag pit," where trainers may force them to continue fighting for hours.

Other animal "athletes" include wrestling bears, diving mules, and boxing kangaroos. Like all performers, these animals spend large parts of their time on the road—often crammed inside tiny cages or stalls.

It is crucial that you and your friends boycott these events whenever they occur. However, to put an end to these activities altogether, see our section on effectively protesting animal-exploitation events, on page 179.

29

Censor Movies and TV Shows Depicting Cruelty to Animals

■

There are a lot of directors who will injure animals to further a plot. I will have none of it.

—James Mason

Avoid movies and television shows whose production caused animals to suffer. Be on the lookout for television shows, films, and adults' or children's books that abuse or demean our animal kin. Voice complaints to the TV networks and their sponsors, local movie houses, bookstores, and public and school libraries.

Please remember that if a filmed, photographed, or videotaped event depicts cruelty to animals, it's likely that the animal was literally abused to produce the segment. After all, how do you make an animal portray pain? Don't you have to hurt it? How do you make animals emote such feelings as anxiety or fear? Don't you have to scare them?

Although a mechanical shark dummy was used in *Jaws*, countless other films, including the all-

118

American Western, involve the unnecessary injuring and annihilation of hundreds of animals each year. Trip wires and other techniques are used to make horses and stunt riders fall over. In fact, until the institution of recent reforms, cowboy movies made in the U.S. accounted for the injury and death of thousands of horses. Most "spaghetti" Westerns made abroad, however, continue to cause much suffering to the animals they use. Few in the audience think twice about seeing a few crocodiles, snakes, or sharks killed for their viewing pleasure. But this carnage constitutes violent, inhumane, and nonessential exploitation of animals.

Films have an indirect effect on animal misuse, as well: The Davy Crockett films, for instance, enabled opportunists to sell coonskin hats made from trapped and shot rabbits, raccoons, and even pet cats. A large bookstore offered heaps of sharks' jaws for sale as an added attraction following the release of *Jaws*.

Remember, boycott and protest all media events that detract from the humane ethic of animal rights. To make complaints about possible cruelty to animals in television or movies, contact the Investigations Division, the American Humane Association, 14144 Ventura Blvd., Sherman Oaks, CA 91423.

We also suggest that you keep prepaid postcards and addresses of major television networks handy so that you can send quick complaints or praise of the station's portrayal of animals. For your convenience, please refer to the following list:

Audience Services
CBS
51 West 52nd Street
New York, NY 10019

Audience Requests
ABC
1330 Avenue of the
  Americas
New York, NY 10019

Audience Services
NBC
30 Rockefeller Plaza
New York, NY 10020

VII
CALL OF THE WILD

30

Become a Rain Forest Refusenik

Animals form an inalienable fragment of nature, and if we hasten
the disappearance of even one species, we diminish our world and
our place in it.

—James Michener

Mother Earth is in great pain—a pain inflicted by her own children
as they commit matricide.

—Rev. Matthew Fox

Avoid the products of rain forest production. For
instance, do not buy furniture made of exotic
woods.

Tropical rain forests, which contain half the
plant and animal species on earth, are now being
destroyed at the rate of fifty acres per minute. This
catastrophic destruction, some scientists estimate,
could lead to the extinction of millions of species
worldwide.

Indeed, the destruction of the rain forests would
not only lead to the extinction of species within the
rain forests—it would cause mass extinctions
around the globe. The reason: These forests are a

vital "lung" for maintaining the atmosphere that we breathe. The rain forests, like all green-plant areas, absorb the carbon dioxide emitted by fossil fuels, people, and animals. As the rain forests shrink, the earth has less ability to absorb and use up carbon dioxide; more carbon dioxide thus accumulates in the atmosphere, trapping solar heat and causing the temperature of the earth to increase (thus the term "greenhouse effect"). As a result, scientists predict severe droughts, crop losses, storms, and floods.

For the animal kingdom, the global greenhouse effect spells suffering, death, and extinction. Unable to reach greener pastures and cool, clear waters, animals will roast inside their fur coats, broil in their burrows, and suffocate in lakes and oceans. Only a few species will be able to migrate to more hospitable habitats, and the competition for these places will be intense, probably resulting in rapid habitat degradation.

To protect the rain forests, do not buy rain forest woods such as mahogany and teak. Instead, stick with alternate woods, including oak, spruce, pine, birch, and beech. Also boycott beef imported from tropical countries. You might even write to fast-food outlets, urging them not to use any rain forest beef.

Finally, to protect rain forests as well as other forests worldwide, we urge you to reduce the number of trees being cut down by recycling paper. (For products sold from recycled paper, send for the *Recycled Paper Catalog* of the Earth Care Paper Co., P. O. Box 3335, Madison, WI 53704.) To help mitigate the impact of the greenhouse effect, reduce the energy you consume as much as you comfortably can.

For more information, contact:

The Rain Forest Action
  Network
300 Broadway
San Francisco, CA
  94133

TERRA (Tropical
  Ecosystem Research
  and Rescue Alliance)
P. O. Box 18391
Washington, DC 20036

The Rain Forest
  Alliance
270 Lafayette St.
Room 512
New York, NY 10012

If you are interested in protecting U.S. forests, 70 percent of which have been destroyed, contact:

The Native Forest
  Council
P. O. Box 2171
Eugene, OR 97402

Earth First!
P. O. Box 5871
Tucson, AZ 85703

(Also ask about this group's publication, *The Radical Environment Journal*.)

To read up on the problem of rain forests and other forests, tap some of the books in the following list:

In the Rain Forest by Catherine Caulfield, Alfred A. Knopf, New York.

Extinction: The Causes and Consequences of the Disappearance of Species by Paul and Anne Ehrlich, Random House, New York, 1984.

Hoofprints on the Forest by Douglas Shane, Institute for the Study of Human Issues, Philadelphia, 1986.

For other book listings, contact:

Abundant Life Seed
  Foundation
P. O. Box 772
Port Townsend, WA
  98368

31

Save the Oceans

If human civilization is going to invade the waters of the earth, then let it be first of all to carry a message of respect.
—Jacques-Yves Cousteau

As we approach the twenty-first century, we are witnessing a massive assault against the seas. One of the most destructive forces may be the practice of modern, factory-scale fishing. For instance, for every ton of shrimp caught, three tons of fish are thrown back into the ocean—after they have already been destroyed. In fact, accidental killing of non-target animals has generated a population decline in sea turtles, dolphins, seals, seabirds, and manatees. More than 1 million sea birds are accidentally killed each year; and an estimated 20,000 porpoises die annually in North Atlantic and Pacific salmon gill nets. Vast, forty-mile-long drift nets are destroying millions of ocean creatures, especially in the Pacific. These "curtains of death" traverse the oceans several times over, killing every marine organism in their path.

Pollution has brought widespread destruction to marine life as well. Coastal wetlands, including estuaries, swamps, salt marshes, and sea-grass meadows, must be protected from pollution and land reclamation for industrial use. Indeed, these areas provide nutrients and habitats for an estimated two-thirds of the world's fisheries, as well as for many marine organisms, including cod, plaice, and herring. Pollution also weakens the immune systems of marine creatures and is a major reason why so many dolphins, seals and whales are dying from various diseases.

Finally, our coral reefs are threatened by offshore drilling, oil spills, industrial pollution, as well as dredging and silting (from increased soil erosion on land).

To help save marine life, you may contact the following organizations:

Greenpeace U.S.A.
Fort Mason, Building E
San Francisco, CA
   94123
       or
1436 U St. NW
Washington, DC 20009

Center for Marine
  Conservation
1725 De Sales Street,
  NW
Washington, DC 20036

American Cetacean
  Society
1300 South Arlington
  Ridge, #614
Arlington, VA 22202

Earth Island
300 Broadway, #28
San Francisco, CA
  94123

   Boycotting all seafood is a mark of personal commitment to the plight of marine life. By joining one
· or more nonprofit organizations devoted to marine
life, you can help to pressure governments at home
and abroad to protect the seas. Through such
groups, you and other members may direct effective political action, probably the single most important step in saving the oceans.

32

Save the Whales

> The difference in mind between man and the higher animals, great as it is, certainly is one of degree and not of kind.
>
> —Charles Darwin

Today, every great species of whale is endangered. If we do not curb our activities, before too long whales will become extinct.

Like the dolphin, the whale is a marine mammal, or cetacean, and one of the most intelligent creatures on earth. We have already discussed dolphins on page 53, under the section entitled "Eat Dolphin-Safe Tuna." But the whales are in desperate trouble, as well.

Back in 1982, when the plight of the whales became especially obvious, the International Whaling Commission (IWC), a group formed by treaty to set quotas for whalers, declared a worldwide moratorium on commercial whaling. The ban was supposed to go into effect in 1986. But three major whaling nations—Japan, Iceland, and Norway—refused to comply. These countries continued to kill thousands of whales, and also declared that they were killing them for a good cause—scientific research. Of course, meat from these whales "killed in the name of science" ended up satisfying the palates of those with a taste for exotic meat.

A subsequent boycott against fish from Iceland caused that country, in 1989, to declare that it would not kill whales in 1990. However, Japan and Norway continue to kill whales for "scientific" purposes, and Iceland may soon join them. In 1990, the IWC voted to continue the moratorium, leading many to fear that whaling nations may just use the ruling as a reason for leaving the IWC.

To help these highly intelligent, endangered marine mammals, you should, of course, avoid eating whale meat at all costs. But more than that, write to President Bush and ask that he impose economic sanctions against outlaw whaling nations. You can also express your concern by calling the White House, at (202) 456-7639. In addition, write to your representative and senators to request that they continue to support and fund a strong Marine Mammal Protection Act.

You can also write to the embassies of the nations still involved in whaling. Tell them you want to see whaling stopped.

Embassy of Iceland
2022 Connecticut
   Avenue NW
Washington, DC 20008

Embassy of Japan
2520 Massachusetts
   Avenue NW
Washington, DC 20008

Embassy of Norway
2720 34th Street NW
Washington, DC 20008

33

Use Artificial Lures

The quaint, old, cruel coxcomb in his gullet
Should have a hook, and a small trout to pull it.

—Lord Byron

All you need to catch a fish is a hook, a line and a stinker.

—John Bryant

If you *must* fish, do not use live bait. If fishing is a sport you cannot give up, use artificial lures, since hooked worms feel pain. Kill the fish humanely as soon as they are caught. Do not let fish struggle and suffer in a bucket or on a stringer. The use of lead sinkers should be prohibited. They can break off and, like the lead shot from duck hunters' guns, can be swallowed by waterbirds and result in death from chronic lead poisoning.

DO FISH HAVE FEELINGS?

Even though fish don't scream when they are in pain and anguish, their behavior should be evidence enough of their suffering when they are hooked or netted. They struggle, endeavoring to escape and, by so doing, demonstrate they have a will to survive—the survival instinct that Albert Schweitzer called the will-to-be.

In fact, thanks to advances in neurochemistry, it has been shown that fish (like other vertebrate animals, including humans) have a highly developed system that may help protect them from severe pain—pain that could be overwhelming enough to endanger their lives. This system releases natural opiatelike substances (enkephalins and endorphins) once an animal is injured. The presence of this pain-dampening opiate system implies that there must be some capacity to experience pain; otherwise, there would be little point in animals having evolved such a system in the first place.

This finding surely confirms what we know intuitively when we allow ourselves to empathize with the desperate struggles of a fish caught on a hook. But is the fish simply in pain? Perhaps it could also be in a state of fear. Indeed, the mental anguish could be far more intense than the pain of a small, sharp hook through a bony lip. According to Dutch researcher John Verheijen and his co-workers, the pain resulting from injury by the hook contributes less to the fish's suffering than fear. This conclusion was reached following comparisons of the behavior of carp after being caught on a hook. Some of the hooked fish were held with a slack line, while others were held with the line pulled taut. In the experiments described in *New Scientist*, April 2, 1987, it was observed that those not held on a taut line ate again soon after release, but those subjected to line pressure avoided food for a considerable time afterwards. After being hooked, the fish darted, dived, spat, and shook their heads, as if trying to expel unwanted food. A few minutes after pressure was applied to the line, the carp began to display a type of behavior called "spitgas," prolonged spitting of gas from the swim bladder, which resulted in their sinking when the line was finally slackened. Additional experiments used electrical currents to produce more precise pain stimuli; after several minutes of exposure, the carp began spitting gas and sinking. Stated Verheijen, "The delay between the painful stimulation and the responses of spitgas and sinking indicated a series of ongoing biochemical and physiological processes associated with fear." The results of the project, supported by the Dutch Society for the Protection of Animals, the Dutch Angling Society, and a government agency, have prompted the Dutch government to promise to investigate further "the cruelty of sport fishing."

Finally, some species of fish change color instantly when alarmed, returning to normal when safely out of danger. Such overt alterations in coloration (analogous to a person turning white with fear) are indicative of internal biochemical changes that mediate emotional reactions, such as panic and escape behavior. To presume that there is no subjective experience or feeling of fear associated with these emotional reactions is illogical.

Indeed, neuroscientists have discovered that all vertebrate animals, including the bony species of fish, have a benzodiazepine receptor system in their brains. This receptor system is blocked by drugs like Valium, which are known to reduce fear and anxiety in humans. This means that fish have the neurochemical system, and thus the brain capacity, to experience fear and anxiety.

Many fish keepers have related how some fish seem to act depressed, becoming pale and lethargic, when separated from their mates. And ethologists have recently shown that sociable fish like goldfish do not thrive so well when deprived of contact with their own kind.

34

Put an End to Hunting

As often as Herman had witnessed the slaughter of animals and fish, he always had the same thought: In their behavior toward creatures, all men were Nazis.

—Isaac Bashevis Singer

(Thus) even in civilized communities, the embryo man passes through the hunter stage of development.

—Henry David Thoreau

"**S**ports" such as trophy-hunting, big-game hunting, and bow-and-arrow hunting should be condemned. Today, almost all hunting is part of a nonsubsistence industry that is ethically and environmentally untenable.

We do not condemn humane subsistence hunting, in which hunters maintain a yield of specific nonendangered species for human consumption. But in the United States and many other areas of the world today, this is usually not the case. For instance, wildlife departments often eliminate natural predators such as the wolf and mountain lion to reduce competition for hunters and ranchers.

Not only does this violate what should be our guiding ethical code, but it also upsets the ecological balance of the earth.

Hunters often twist this argument around by insisting that sport hunting actually maintains ecological balance. For instance, many hunters insist that it is in the interests of animal welfare to shoot deer or other animals rather than let them starve in winter. These hunters never mention—indeed, they may not know—that deer, elk, and other ungulates are physiologically and behaviorally adapted to cope with seasonal starvation.

What's more, certain animals, such as the lynx and bobcat, can simply never adapt to human predation. Unlike coyotes, their reproductive rate does not increase in response to deaths caused by hunting and trapping; unregulated human activities can therefore lead to localized species extinction.

In short, the notion that hunting maintains ecological balance is a myth. Even in areas where this seems to be true, it is because wildlife management schemes have created the very overpopulation that hunting is supposed to control. What's more, unlike predators, which tend to stalk weak, sick, and old animals, hunters usually go after the healthiest individuals, leaving the least viable individuals as breeding stock. In instances in which game agencies keep waterfowl in unnaturally crowded conditions, thousands may die in a single outbreak of disease. Finally, ecosystems created especially for hunters always seem to include deer, pheasants, and waterfowl. This is in contrast to healthy *natural* systems, which depend on the subtle interaction of myriad plant and animal species.

We particularly protest the more inhumane methods of hunting, including bow hunting and trapping. Bow hunting is often inaccurate, and may leave an animal alive and suffering for hours or days. The steel leghold trap, responsible for the maiming and death of some 200 million animals in the U.S. each year, causes untold suffering. Not only do the traps inflict excruciating pain, but trap lines are often left unchecked for forty-eight hours or more. (For a listing of live traps, which you may use to remove wildlife from your property, see page 26.) No matter what the method of hunting, moreover, most recreational hunters are not experienced enough to inflict a clean kill, downing the animal with one well-placed shot. Instead, many hunted animals are merely wounded. And statistics show that as many as 50 percent of wounded animals are left to bleed to death or succumb slowly to gangrene and infection.

Especially horrific are "shooting preserves," which sell hunters the opportunity to shoot semi-tame or confined animals for a fee. The 3,000 U.S. preserves stock everything from game birds to exotic animals, depending on the facility. In some preserves, the hunter is actually driven by Jeep to the very spot at which the prey is eating its daily handout of food.

To help end the sport of hunting, we suggest that you substitute any hunting activities with such hobbies as bird-watching, nature photography, or hiking and camping in the woods. If you have children, be sure to take them on hiking and camping trips so that they may learn to appreciate the beauty and value of wildlife.

If you yourself own wooded, rural property, put up signs that say *No Hunting or Trapping*. Suggest that your friends and neighbors put up such signs, as well. Ask local police or game wardens to help enforce your prohibition.

When you find evidence or personally witness infractions by hunters—for instance, if you see a whole deer carcass left in the woods; if you see hunters shooting animals from a car or truck on a public road, or hunting at night by spotlight—contact the local game warden. After all, hunters should at least be forced to follow the rules that now exist.

Check to see if your state has a program for conserving non-game wildlife. If not, contact your congressman and senators and ask that they support this sort of program in your area. It's also important to protest hunting programs permitted in America's valuable wildlife refuges, many of which have become killing grounds. Each year, the U.S. Fish and Wildlife Service permits hunters to shoot and trap hundreds of thousands of animals on these supposedly sacred preserves. According to the latest statistics, 146,000 animals are trapped and 500,000 shot on 400 refuges nationwide. To prevent this federally sponsored slaughter, write your U.S. representative and senators, urging that they sponsor and support actively any legislation to abolish hunting and trapping in the National Wildlife Refuge System. In your letters, ask them to help restore our nation's refuges to the places of protection they were intended to be. Insist that you no longer wish to be deprived of *your* right to *enjoy* refuge wildlife.

If you are interested in an especially direct form of action, you may organize your neighbors to buy up all the hunting permits in your community, then throw them away. You can also disrupt a hunt in progress by making a lot of noise and driving creatures away. This effective and nonviolent form of civil disobedience could get you arrested, however, since hunters have won legal protection under the Hunter Harassment Law, now in effect in almost forty states.

Sanctioned violence in the name of agriculture is extensive and extreme. In 1989, for instance, the Animal Control Division of the U.S. Department of Agriculture spent $29 million to hunt, trap, and shoot coyotes, bobcats, and mountain lions living near livestock. Many other species are killed as a result of this program, as well.

Biologists have recently shown that the Animal Damage Control program is a complete waste of public funds. Coyotes have more offspring when their numbers are reduced, and quickly colonize any area where their own kind have been exterminated. Mountain lions, bobcats, grizzly bears, and wolves are not so adaptable, but they, like coyotes, help control rabbits and rodents that compete for forage with livestock. The extermination of these creatures is especially criminal because our use of meat is excessive and unhealthy, constituting nonsustainable overconsumption. To protest the Animal Damage Control program, write to your congressional representative. Ask that the current program be replaced with non-lethal methods of predator control.

35

Leave Wild Creatures in the Wilderness, Where They Belong

Resist the temptation to take wild creatures like lizards, turtles, and non-venomous snakes home as pets. All wild creatures should be respected; that respect must encompass their right to be left in the wild—the only place where they can live in accordance with their natural inclinations and abilities.

We also urge you to resist *buying* exotic or wild pets from pet stores or any other source. Those who sell such pets—including monkeys, parrots, macaws, cockatoos, or raccoons—may try to convince you that anyone with patience and sensitivity can raise a wild animal at home. They may even tell you that you can help the cause of endangered wildlife by buying two such animals and *breeding* them. These claims are myths. The truth is that the hundreds of thousands of wild animals caught and marketed as pets each year will remain wild no matter where and how they are raised. Raccoons, for instance, will always be nocturnal creatures who are frightened—and sometimes rendered dangerous—by strange sights and sounds. Skunks, now being de-scented and sold as pets, may carry rabies. In one instance, a Capuchin monkey weighing in at about twenty pounds suddenly attacked and killed a four-year-old boy. These creatures are unsuitable for home rearing and handling, often ill when purchased, and likely to die shortly after they enter captivity. This fact is underscored by the number of prestigious organizations that have spoken out against keeping wild animals as pets. These include the American Veterinary Medical Association, the Centers for Disease Control, the American Association of Zoological Parks and Aquariums, as well as many state veterinary groups.

Once these creatures have been made into pets, however, think twice about relocating them back into the wild. Animals that have become attached to people, or carnivores that do not know how to hunt, may not adapt when released. Be forewarned, however: Zoos may not want your discarded exotic or wild pet, either. When raised in a home by people who are not experts in animal care, exotic and wild animals are often in poor health, overly temperamental, and unable to socialize with their own species. Unfortunately, for these creatures euthanasia may be the only solution.

Instead of putting your time and money into the ownership of a wild or exotic animal, we suggest that you put these same resources toward saving the wilderness areas that remain.

36

Only Buy Birds Born and Raised in Captivity—If You Must

> Buy captive creatures and set them free.
>
> —Yin-Chih-wen

Each year, some 30 million birds are captured from the wild. Of these, 22½ million die brutal deaths due to vicious capture techniques, injuries, inadequate care, starvation, and shock. Shipped from native lands, hundreds of birds are often packed in crates meant for two or three dozen and left without food or water for days. Overly stressed, the birds often start fighting with one another and many are injured or killed. Many birds often succumb to disease. It is not unusual, in shipments of 3,000 or 4,000, to have every single bird arrive dead. After all is said and done, only 7½ million of the original 30 million birds arrive at their destination alive.

To end this abuse, the real answer lies in putting a ban on the commercial sale of birds caught in the wild. In fact, we urge you to buy only birds bred in captivity if you must keep a bird in a cage. Ideally, no bird should be caged alone, since all birds are social creatures. In fact, we suggest that bird companions have the freedom of a safe room or enclosed porch. Captive-bred and raised birds, which are tame and bred to have placid dispositions, make far better companions than wild-caught ones. Remember, a tame, friendly bird that enjoys the company of people will be a lot more pleasant to have around than a stressed, neurotic, angry, and sick bird that has been imported.

For your information, there is widespread support for a ban on commercial trade in wild birds. The Convention on International Trade in Endangered Species of Fauna and Flora (CITES) currently advocates an international treaty banning trade in wild birds. Among the groups also supporting such a ban are The American Veterinary Medical Association, the Humane Society of the United States, the Animal Welfare Institute, the American Society for the Prevention of Cruelty to Animals, the Animal Protection Institute, the Fund for Animals, Defenders of Wildlife, and the National Audubon Society.

Become an Ecotourist

The natural world is the larger sacred community to which we belong. To be alienated from this community is to become destitute in all that makes us human.

—Father Thomas Berry

Take a vacation that brings you closer to nature and wildlife. As we have suggested throughout this book, you will come to empathize more with animals if you have the chance to observe them in their natural environment. For instance, you may go on a camping trip to Lake Tahoe or the Grand Canyon, and while there take up such activities as nature photography or bird-watching.

For those interested in especially unusual or exotic nature trips, we suggest that you look into the burgeoning field of ecological tourism, or *ecotourism*, for short. Thanks to this increasingly popular subdivision of the travel industry, responsible tours to jungles, wild lands, and natural habitats go to great lengths to avoid causing any negative environmental impact. Not only will such trips enable you to explore many unusual natural habitats, but they also will help literally to preserve ecosystems in the Third World. Indeed, as one of the top industries in Africa, ecotourism has generated significant income, providing economic alternatives to burning and slashing the rain forests for agriculture and cattle raising, or slaughtering elephants for their tusks.

Remember, if you do decide to have the ecotourism industry help you plan your next trip, be careful to make sure that you have gotten involved with a responsible group. After all, irresponsible tourism in the Third World and elsewhere has led to the *destruction* of ecosystems. Rain forests and farmlands, for instance, have been cleared away for golf courses; resorts and hotels have sometimes been built with funds slated for agricultural and economic growth; and four-wheel-drive vehicles and motorcycles have ripped up virgin land that could take as long as a hundred years to revegetate.

Following is a guide to responsible ecotourism organizations:

Biological Journeys, 1867 Ocean Drive, McKinleyville, CA 95521; (415) 527-9622. Specializes in whale watching and other expeditions to observe wildlife along the west coasts of the U.S. and Mexico. For serious environmentalists.

Center for Responsible Tourism, 2 Kensington Road, San Anselmo, CA 94960. For a $10 membership fee, this group will help you plan your trip so that you do no damage to the ecosystems of the Third World.

The Cousteau Society, 930 West 21st Street, Norfolk, VA 23517; (804) 627-1144. For a summer work-vacation studying marine ecosystems, you can apply for a job diving or doing other useful work through the Cousteau Society.

Earthwatch, 680 Mount Auburn Street, P. O. Box 403, Watertown, MA 02172; (617) 926-8200. This organization will send you on a volunteer vacation to study the various cultures and/or ecosystems of the planet Earth. The work is hard, but participants come away having learned and grown a lot.

University Research Expedition Program, c/o University of California at Berkeley, Desk G-8, Berkeley, CA 94720; (415) 624-6586. This group will send you on a research expedition with a university group, studying such areas as marine biology, ecology, and zoology.

In addition, many environmental organizations—from the Sierra Club to the Audubon Society and the Nature Conservancy—run travel programs. These programs are environmentally sound, and the profits they generate go toward conservation efforts.

For updated travel opportunities, see the environmental journal *Buzzworm*, 1818 16th Street, Boulder, CO 80302.

You may also be interested in registering for a course with a wilderness school. Some of the best include:

Boulder Outdoor
  Survival School
P. O. Box 905
Rexburg, ID 83440

National Outdoor
  Leadership School
P. O. Box AA
Lander, WY 82520

Outward Bound
  Schools
384 Field Point Road
Greenwich, CT 06830

Reevis Mountain School
HCO2
Box 1534
Globe, AZ 85501

The Tracker School
P. O. Box 173
Asbury, NJ 07702

VIII
THE COMMUNITY OF CONSCIENCE

38

Share Your Convictions About Animals with Everyone

Non-human creatures are not merely objects to be used for our pleasure or instruments for human purposes, but are of value in themselves and to God. . . .

—World Council of Churches

Explain the importance of animal welfare and rights to all your friends and neighbors.

Ask your religious leader to talk about human responsibility toward animals at upcoming services in your place of worship. If you are interested, you can even deliver talks and become a leader in your religious community yourself. To acquire resource and liturgical materials suitable for presentation to congregations of all faiths, contact the Center for Respect of Life and Environment, 2100 L Street NW, Washington, DC 20037, and the Interfaith Council for Protection of Animals and Nature, 4290 Raintree Lane NW, Atlanta, GA 30327. You can also find guidance in the book *Only One Earth,* published by the United Nations Environment Program, United Nations, Room DC 2-803, New York, NY 10017.

Express your views in local newspapers, and encourage local radio, television, or cable stations to produce an animal community news segment devoted to such issues as pet care and urban wildlife. The shows can also help to locate lost pets or advertise animals up for adoption.

Talk to your local store managers and grocers and ask them to carry organic produce, humane, range-free eggs, natural organic beef, and tofu. Ask them to eliminate glue traps from their racks. Talk to the hairdressers and manicurists around town and ask them to sell products that have not been tested on animals.

Encourage friends to support local health-food coops and farmers' markets, as well as organic farm cooperatives.

Carry animal-rights literature, including anti-fur pamphlets and leaflets warning against leaving animals in hot cars. Distribute the literature to your friends, and leave pamphlets in local stores, houses of worship, community centers, buses, taxicabs, and even the laundromat. You can also arrange to set up an animal-rights information booth at your local shopping mall each month. If you and your friends are able to set up such a booth, remember to bring a TV set and VCR so that you can show videotapes on animal cruelty.

Animals share with us the privilege of having a soul.

—Pythagoras

To obtain appropriate literature and video material, including public-service announcements for local TV and camera-ready advertisements for local papers, we suggest that you join a large, national animal-protection organization. Recommended groups include:

Animal Welfare Institute, P. O. Box 3650, Washington, DC 20007; (202) 337-2333.

The Humane Society of the United States, 2100 L Street NW, Washington, DC 20037; (202) 452-1100 (publishes bimonthly *News;* also publishes *Animal Activist Alert*, a regular review of animal legislative protection activities at state and federal levels, published quarterly, free to members on request).

National Alliance for Animal Legislation, P. O. Box 75116, Washington, DC 20013; (703) 684-0654 (grassroots network of individuals that lobbies for animal-protection legislation).

People for the Ethical Treatment of Animals, P. O. Box 42516, Washington, DC 20015-0516; (301) 770-7444 (publishes bimonthly *News*).

World Society for the Protection of Animals, P. O. Box 190, 29 Perkins Street, Boston, MA 02130; (617) 522-7000.

To stay informed enough to inform others, we recommend that you read one or more of the following periodicals:

Animals' Advocate newsletter, published by The Animal Legal Defense Fund (a nationwide network of over 200 attorneys), 1363 Lincoln Ave., San Rafael, CA 94901.

The Animals' Agenda—The Animal Rights Magazine, P. O. Box 5234, Westport, CT 06881.

The Animals' Voice (a glossy animal-rights magazine), P. O. Box 5312, Beverly Hills, CA 90209-5312

E—The Environmental Magazine, published by Earth Action Network, 20 Knight Street, Norwalk, CT 06851.

Earth Island Journal (International Environmental News), published by Earth Island Institute, 300 Broadway, Suite 28, San Francisco, CA 94133.

Greenpeace magazine, published by Greenpeace, P. O. Box 3720, 1436 U Street NW, Washington, DC 20007.

Three other informative professional organizations concerned with animal rights are:

Association of Veterinarians for Animal Rights, P. O. Box 6269, Vaca-
    ville, CA 95696
Psychologists for the Ethical Treatment of Animals, Dr. Kenneth Sha-
    piro, coordinator, P. O. Box 87, New Gloucester, ME 04260.
Physicians' Committee for Responsible Medicine, P. O. Box 6322,
    Washington, DC 20015.

We also suggest that you check out and consider supporting your local humane society.

39

Convince Schools to Give a Course in Animal-Human Relations

If you are thinking a year ahead, sow seed. If you are thinking ten years ahead, plant a tree. If you are thinking one hundred years ahead, educate the people.

—Chinese proverb

Approach your local school board or school administrators and ask them to incorporate a course in human-animal relations into the curriculum. Depending on the age of the students and experience of teachers available, this type of course may cover such topics as: animals' rights; man's domestication of nature; cruelty and kindness; the morality of zoos; eating with conscience and the school cafeteria menu; genetically engineered animals; animals in entertainment; pet behavior; and the use of animals in research, agriculture, medicine, and in school biology classes. You might even acquire recordings of animal sound and language, demonstrating to students that animals communicate with meaning and nuance, much as we do.

When you argue for the inclusion of a course on animals, explain to administrators that groups such as the National Rifle Association (NRA) have for years spent millions of dollars teaching children that hunting and trapping are necessary to maintain the environment—a point of view that is erroneous. Humane education, on the other hand, has been more or less neglected in the U.S., and continues to be opposed by such vested interest groups as the NRA, American Farm Bureau Federation, and the American Medical Association. Enlightened educators keep such influences out of the classroom.

You might also point out that even in cities, we are constantly surrounded by pets and urban wildlife. These animals have adapted to the changes that we have imposed on the natural world. We owe it to them—and to the rest of nature—at least to *think* about our impact on the earth.

Finally, while you are advocating humane education, we suggest that you also oppose dissection in your neighborhood schools. If that effort fails, pass around a petition advocating each student's right to choose whether or not to participate in dissection without being penalized.

For guidance on developing an animal curriculum of your own, we suggest you contact the National Association for Humane and Environmental Education (NAHEE), 67 Salem Road, East Haddam, CT 06423; (203) 434-8666.

For $18 a year, you can also join the Adopt-A-Teacher Program established by NAHEE. As a member, you will receive extensive humane materials, which you can then supply to the school library or teacher of your choice. NAHEE can also help high school and college students start animal- or environmental-protection clubs in or out of school.

You need not use these resource materials only in conventional grade schools or high schools. If your local school district fails to respond, try to set up a humane education course through church groups, the Boy Scouts or Girl Scouts, 4-H clubs, Rotary clubs, Sunday schools, or adult-education centers.

If you are a university graduate, you can use your clout as an alumnus to influence school policies in favor of animals; for instance, you and other alumni who contribute to your alma mater might even threaten to withdraw financial support if harmful policies concerning lab animals used for research and teaching purposes do not change.

We also suggest that you lobby for humane education in your state.

40

Stay on the Lookout for Animals That May Need Your Help

To think out in every implication the ethic of love for all creation—
this is the difficult task which confronts our age.

—Albert Schweitzer

Become aware of your surroundings. Notice and
help injured animals lying by the side of the road,
a miserable dog chained in a neighbor's yard, or a
wild animal roaming without food in extreme
weather. In the case of the wild animal, you may
simply scatter food in a given area until the
weather improves. In especially treacherous situa-
tions, make sure to call in the appropriate people
to assist you. If you find an injured or obviously
orphaned wild animal, do not attempt to care for
it yourself. These animals need expert care in order
to thrive and ultimately be introduced back into
the wild. To make sure injured or orphaned animals
get such care, hand them over to your local humane
society, animal-control agency, or wildlife rehabilitation center.

We also suggest that you monitor variety stores that may sell pets, as well as pet stores, local animal auction yards, county fairs, and visiting circuses for animal neglect and cruelty. If you notice a sick animal for sale, or if you see a litter of kittens broiling behind the plate-glass in glaring sun, contact your local animal-control and health departments, as well as your local humane society. Also call your state department of consumer affairs and report suspicions of deceptive business practices.

While you're examining your community, it may also be a good idea for you to organize your neighbors to investigate municipal spraying of trees and roadside vegetation with pesticides; depending on the degree of spraying, this activity may need to be regulated or stopped. Examine your local park—it should not be mowed completely. Make sure park managers allow some grass and wildflower areas to grow. Check on local industries that may be causing pollution of rivers or other wildlife habitats, and pressure them and city hall to clean up or clear out.

For up-to-date information on the care of abandoned, homeless, or abused pets in your community, we suggest that you subscribe to *Shelter Sense*, published by the Humane Society of the United States, 4530 Grosvenor Lane, Suite 100, Bethesda MD 20814. Also write to *Shelter Sense* for a free brochure on making your cat an indoor animal.

Save the Worms

Even in the worm that crawls in the earth there glows a divine spark. When you slaughter a creature, you slaughter God.

—Isaac Bashevis Singer

Look out for worms on the sidewalk after it rains. Teach children to follow the example of St. Francis of Assisi, who would pick up such creatures and put them back in the grass.

42

Be a Responsible Pet Owner

■

I care not for a man's religion whose dog and cat are not the better for it.

—Abraham Lincoln

Following are some helpful tips that will aid you in your attempts to become a responsible companion animal owner:

- Don't let your pet roam free. Animals that roam through communities on their own are exposed to such things as sick animals, rabies, ticks (and Lyme disease), canine distemper, and, in the case of cats, feline AIDS. Roaming pets may also be hit by cars, shot by hunters, caught in traps, and stolen to be sold to research laboratories. Keeping tabs on your pets will also serve to protect wildlife. Cats, for instance, can kill birds and small mammals; dogs can mangle sheep.
- Set up an outdoor pen or enclosed patio for your cats.

162   You Can Save the Animals

- Do not chain your dog up all day in the yard; it will get lonely and bark incessantly.
- Provide your companion animals with preventive veterinary care, as well as with other appropriate veterinary care when needed.
- Spay or neuter your pet. If your pet hasn't been neutered and is free-roaming, it could well become pregnant and the offspring would add to the millions of unwanted dogs and cats put to death each year. Spaying or neutering your pets will also reduce the possibility of illness and injury, and make them better companions because they will be less motivated to go out and roam in search of a mate. Eighty percent of the dogs hit by automobiles are unaltered males. Spayed and neutered animals are also far less likely to suffer from cancer and many other forms of disease.

We also suggest that all pet owners remember the 6 "R's" of responsible pet care:

1. *Right understanding*, which involves knowing the animal's behavioral repertoire of body-language symbols used to express needs and intentions.
2. *Right rearing*, in which animals are taught to socialize with humans during critical periods in early life. (In the case of dogs and cats, for instance, this is between six and ten weeks of age.)
3. *Right environment*, in which the emotional and physical elements of the animal's environment are developed with care. For instance, whenever possible, animals should be provided with the company of at least one of their own kind. Additional environmental provisions include regular periods of grooming and play for cats and dogs.

4. *Right breeding*, in which cats and dogs are selectively bred to be healthy and have stable temperaments. (For more on this, see page 165, on the problems of pedigree pets.)
5. *Right nutrition*, in which owners provide companion animals with a wholesome, balanced diet.

Additional rights include the right to appropriate veterinary treatment when sick, regular (at least annual) veterinary health check-ups, and the right to humane euthanasia when a pet is too old or sick to be able to enjoy life.

Finally, we suggest that before you buy a pet, you make sure its breed and temperament are compatible with your life-style. An active working breed like a malamute or border collie does not adapt well to a sedentary suburban existence or to being left alone all day in an apartment. Regardless of breed, many other dogs also suffer from confinement, boredom, and separation from their human companions who are away at work all day.

43

Adopt Pound Puppies and Shelter Cats

We and the beasts are kin.

—Ernest Thompson Seton

Find your pets through the pound, an animal shelter, or a responsible local breeder. Always buy your pets from humane sources, and refrain from patronizing puppy mills—mass dog-breeding establishments—or the pet stores that buy the animals that they produce. Many puppy mills are known for their cruel and inhumane conditions, with infractions that include overcrowding; filth; exposure to the elements; insufficient food, water, and veterinary care. Breeding dogs live lives of misery, and are generally "put to sleep" at the age of five or six years, when they are no longer productive. Because breeding parents are not particularly well cared for or monitored for genetic diseases, puppies produced at puppy mills may not necessarily be healthy. And because puppies are sent from puppy mills to pet stores during their most vulnerable period of development, social and emotional adjustment to people and to surroundings can be permanently disrupted.

If you *must* have a purebred dog or cat, do not patronize pet stores and the puppy mills that they support. Instead, purchase your pet from one of the hundreds of responsible and reputable kennels and breeding establishments throughout the United States. If you wish to purchase a pet from one of these establishments, by all means *visit* to make sure the animal you will be taking home was raised in good and healthy surroundings. Insist that you meet the parents of the dog you will be buying.

Encourage any friends in the market for a dog to visit a local animal shelter, where they can adopt a homeless pet. Also drop by the local pet store and ask the manager where the puppies come from. If the dogs come from out of state, or if the owner seems unsure about breeding conditions, suggest that he or she patronize only reputable breeders, particularly those in the area.

Perhaps most important, we urge you to buy a mixed-breed dog or cat as opposed to a pedigree. Purebred cats and dogs constitute a problem population. These designer animals, bred by humans for as long as several centuries, carry genetic defects that inflict lifelong suffering, sickness, and physical handicaps.

Certain handicaps have become breed standards. For instance, the pushed-in (brachycephalic) face of the bulldog and Persian cat makes it extremely difficult for the animals to breathe normally. Their protruding eyes and facial skin folds become easily infected. The bulldog's disproportionately large soft palate sets up a negative pressure such that the animal's windpipe constricts, or collapses, and the animal is either partially or completely asphyxiated. The standard for large heads in these two breeds means that many newborns cannot pass through the mother's birth canal, making Cesarian sections routine. Sloping hindquarters in breeds like the German shepherd are linked with hip dysplasia, a crippling disease. And extremely pendulous ears in cocker spaniels are linked to distressing, lifelong ear infections.

Inbreeding also contributes to an increased incidence of all types of genetic disease. The reason: a narrow genetic base, in which sisters breed with grandfathers and uncles, and half-sisters with half-brothers. Some of the genetic problems found in purebred dogs include dwarfism, giantism, epilepsy, deafness, cataracts, glaucoma, progressive blindness, increased rate of slipped disks and kneecap dislocation, progressive muscular weakness, and progressive renal disease. Other problems include increased incidence of cancer and brain tumors, dental problems, arthritis and lameness (especially in dwarfed breeds with shortened legs like the basset hound), Perth's disease, hemophilia, hysteria, extreme fearfulness, hyperactivity, autoimmune diseases, and reduced resistance to diseases and infection in general.

Some purebreds have the added insult and affliction of ear cropping, an unnecessary and painful operation, as part of their breed's standard to have erect ears. The practice should be eliminated.

We want to point out that although cats have only recently been subjected to the kind of intensive breeding going on for generations in dogs, the pedigree feline is now beginning to show drastically increased evidence of serious, inherited diseases of its own. These include head deformities in the Burmese breed, hemophilia in the British shorthair, spasticity in the Devon Rex, spina bifida in Manx cats, and cardiac myopathy in Abyssinians.

The selective inbreeding problem in both cats and dogs is further compounded by the phenomenon of "overbreeding," in which a popular breed is mass-produced for the pet market without any "quality control." That is, breeders fail to follow up on these animals to see whether they are breeding from stock that has transmitted genetic disorders on to the offspring. Little wonder, then, that owners of puppy-mill-bred animals are at a loss when their six-month-old Samoyed turns out to be crippled with hip dysplasia, or when their cocker spaniel is blind at the age of one year.

Because these animals are purebred, pedigree registration papers can be obtained from the American Kennel Club. This gives owners a false sense of security. Indeed, the AKC has taken no stand whatsoever to prevent the registration of genetically defective animals. Through local and national organizations, however, concerned owners of purebred dogs have begun to try to set up standards and registries of their own.

Diseased pedigree animals exist mostly because of human ignorance, egotistical self-indulgence, and commercial greed. Pedigree animals will continue to suffer, moreover, until breeders and the American Kennel Club take a more responsible attitude. In light of this, we urge all prospective dog and cat owners to refrain from buying a purebred companion animal. Instead, we suggest that you make the ethical—and fashionable—choice of a mongrel, or mixed breed, animal.

If you dislike the notion of a mutt, it is also acceptable to have as your animal companion a first- or second-generation hybrid—essentially, the cross between two or four pedigree animals. For instance, one may breed the cross between a golden retriever and a pointer with the cross between a German shepherd and a collie. Some mixes, like

the cockerpoo (cocker spaniel and poodle) and pu-
lipoo (puli and poodle) and shitpoo (shitzu and
poodle), are popular, as well.

GENETIC DEFECTS IN PUREBRED ANIMALS

Defect	Number of breeds affected
Cataracts	16
Progressive retinal atrophy	28
Glaucoma	9
Entropion (turning inward of eyelashes)	24
Ectropion (turning outward of lower eyelid)	10
Deafness	14
Hip dysplasia	35
Hemophilia	25
Cardiovascular disorders	26
Cleft palate	19
Female reproductive dysfunctions	15
Epilepsy	17

44

Become a Volunteer

It is better to give than to receive.

—Anon.

Volunteer to help your local Humane Society or animal shelter run kennels and veterinary clinics, facilitate animal adoptions, and provide humane education programs.

If volunteer work is your goal, the organizations and magazines listed on page 153 will provide you with much supportive information. We also suggest that you check in your state to locate a large and effective animal-protection organization such as: the Massachusetts SPCA, 450 Salem End Road, P. O. Box 2314, Framingham Centre, MA 07101; the Marin County Humane Society, 171 Bell Marin Keys Boulevard, Novato, CA 94947; Peninsula Humane Society, 12 Airport Boulevard, San Mateo, CA 94401; and the New York State Humane Association, P. O. Box 284, New Paltz, NY 12561.

We also suggest that you contact the regional field office of the Humane Society of the United

States nearest you. These groups will help you locate local humane societies and other dedicated people in your immediate community. They can also update you on burning animal-welfare issues in need of community action.

━━━━━━━━━━━━━━━━━━━━━━━━━━━━

Humane Society Regional Field Offices

GREAT LAKES REGIONAL OFFICE
745 Haskins Street
Bowling Green, OH 43402-1696
(419) 352-5141
(419) 354-5351 (FAX)

SERVES: OH, IN, MI, WV
Sandra (Sandy) Rowland,
    Director
Robin Weirauch, Program
    Coordinator
Barbara Matthews, Secretary

GULF STATES REGIONAL OFFICE
6262 Weber Road, Suite 305
Corpus Christi, TX 78413
(512) 854-3142 (854-5922; private)
(512) 854-5922 (FAX)

SERVES: AR, LA, OK, TX
James Noe, Program
    Coordinator
Barbara Nespodzany,
    Administrative Assistant

MID-ATLANTIC REGIONAL OFFICE
Bartley Square
270 Route 206
Flanders, NJ 07836
(201) 927-5611
(201) 927-5617 (FAX)

SERVES: DE, NJ, NY, PA
Virginia (Nina) Austenberg,
    Director
Adelle Dooner, Administrative
    Assistant

MIDWEST REGIONAL OFFICE
Argyle Building
306 East 12th Street, Suite 625
Kansas City, MO 64106
(816) 474-0888
(816) 474-0898 (FAX)

SERVES: MO, KS, NE, IA
Wendell Maddox, Director
Rochelle Bright, Secretary

NEW ENGLAND REGIONAL OFFICE
Norma Terris Center
67A Salem Road
P. O. Box 362 (mail address)
East Haddam, CT 06423
(203) 434-1940
(203) 434-1790 (FAX)

SERVES: CT, MA, ME, NH, RI, VT
Frank Ribaudo, Program
  Coordinator
Sandra Tryon, Secretary

NORTH CENTRAL REGIONAL OFFICE
2015 175th Street
Lansing, IL 60438
(708) 474-0906
(708) 474-9449 (FAX)

SERVES: ND, SD, IL, MN, WI
Frantz Dantzler, Director
Sandra (Sandy) Porter,
  Secretary

SOUTH CENTRAL REGIONAL OFFICE
109 Northshore Drive, Suite 400
Knoxville, TN 37919
(615) 588-1843
(615) 588-1862 (FAX)

SERVES: TN, KY, NC, VA
Phillip Snyder, Director
Angelia McMillian, Secretary

SOUTHEAST REGIONAL OFFICE*
1624 Metropolitan Circle, Suite B
Tallahassee, FL 32303
(904) 386-3435
(904) 386-4534 (FAX)

SERVES: FL, AL, GA, SC, MS
Marc Paulhus, Director
Laura Bevan, Program
  Coordinator
Ken Johnson, Investigator
Andrea Mitchell, Secretary

WEST COAST REGIONAL OFFICE
5301 Madison Avenue, Suite 202
P. O. Box 417220 (mail address)
Sacramento, CA 95841-7220
(916) 344-1710
(916) 344-1808 (FAX)

SERVES: CA, ID, OR, NV, WA
Charlene (Char) Drennon,
  Director
Eric Sakach, Investigator
Kurt Lapham, Investigator
Christin Rogers, Administrative
  Assistant
Patricia Frank, Secretary

Other, independent volunteer efforts might include:

- Setting up a community network of volunteers to care for lost and abandoned dogs and cats in "halfway homes".
- Establishing a neighborhood people-pets partnership program, in which responsible schoolchildren visit elderly and handicapped neighbors and walk their dogs or help care for their birds or cats.
- Starting a "pet-therapy" program, in which pet owners with suitable pets visit retirement homes and hospitals for chronically and terminally ill children and adults. The therapeutic value of pets helps increase public respect for all creatures.
- Raising funds for the shelter of homeless dogs and cats. You can generate enough money for a local animal shelter through such activities as bake sales, yard sales, and door-to-door fundraising. (Some of the money may also go to fund spay-neuter programs to help reduce pet overpopulation.)
- Cleaning and restoring local woodlands, streams, and creeks.

45

Remember Animals in Your Will

■

For that which befalleth the sons of men befalleth beasts;—Yea, they have all one breath; so that man hath no preeminence above a beast: for all is Vanity.

—Ecclesiastes 3:19–20

Write or rewrite your will so that some of the money helps protect animals from cruelty and suffering. Toward this end, you may consider many options, from donating the money to a local or national animal-protection agency to providing a fund for a humane curriculum in your city's schools.

We suggest that you check out a few animal-welfare groups before you choose the one you'd like to support. One way to compare organizations is to ask them for policy statements, performance reports, project lists and financial statements. Never donate large amounts of money to a humane organization that does not provide a financial statement, complete with details of income, expenses, assets, and liabilities. Also request a copy of the organization's bylaws, and make sure you deem them democratic. Though we urge you to check out all the details yourself before donating money to any group, you might start your investigation with the list of fine organizations provided on page 153 of this book.

Once you have chosen an organization, careful tax-planning methods are a must. Outright bequests of money or property will help a group most quickly. However, if you must also use the money to provide for surviving relatives or a spouse, you can put the money in trust for the charity. The income from the trust can be used to support the surviving individual, but upon that person's death, the money goes to the charity. If you own a suitable piece of land, you might consider donating it to an environmental organization for use as a nature preserve.

One last point: if you do decide to donate your money to animal welfare, we urge you to do so with few restrictions. After all, the organization you endow will be forced to abide by your directions into perpetuity; meanwhile, there may be devastating animal-welfare problems that you simply were not able to foresee.

Money left to humane organizations is crucial. Without these bequests, few humane organizations could continue their programs, let alone expand for the future. You may wish to initiate a program in your, or your deceased spouse's name; you may wish to fund a building, a program in humane education or a facility to help rehabilitate wild animals. Note: If you plan to join or give money to a local or national wildlife or conservation organization, be sure to check out their policy on hunting, since many are still pro-hunting, pro-fishing, and even pro-trapping.

Also please be aware of the fact that *many charity*

organizations committed to various human health problems, from birth defects to cancer and heart disease, *support animal research*. Providing them with funds may therefore be contrary to your wishes and beliefs.

Remember, consult a lawyer regarding your plans, and have that attorney involved in any will that you change or write.

IX
THE POLITICAL ANIMAL

Effectively Protest Animal Exploitation

To say one species has a *right* to exploit the others is to be guilty of the prejudice of *speciesism*, just as to argue that one race has a right to subordinate another race is *racism*.
—Richard D. Ryder

Boycotting events such as pulling contests, greased-pig contests, or live-turkey drops from airplanes is not enough. To keep these animal-exploitation events out of your community, follow these steps:

- Find out about events as early as possible. The earlier you protest, the greater your chances of causing the event to be canceled. To keep on top of things, watch advertisements and events listings in local publications and listen to radio announcements.
- Before you come forward with your protest, find out if the event violates local and state anticruelty laws. Call your state game agency to learn if the species involved is protected by law.

- Contact the event sponsor, town, county, and fair officials and tell them about the cruelties intrinsic to the particular sport. If a pulling contest has already been scheduled, contact the fair management, the chamber of commerce, and the media and express your concerns. You might even suggest substitute events, such as marathons, bicycle races, or Frisbee contests.
- If those in charge of the event don't back down, draft a strong letter and send it to local news media, government officials, and enforcement authorities such as game wardens or animal-control officers. Send a copy of the letter to any group sponsoring or benefiting from the event.
- If the letter does not have the desired effect, personally get in touch with television and newspaper reporters and ask that they run a story on the controversy surrounding the upcoming event. The story will have a better chance of appearing if you suggest photo possibilities.
- If the event occurs, organize signed petitions and pickets to protest and invite the media to come. However, check out all local ordinances pertaining to demonstrations before moving forward. The right to engage in acts of nonviolent civil disobedience (like having a demonstration in front of a local store that sells furs, wild-caught parrots, or milk-fed veal, for instance) is protected under the Constitution of the United States.
- Press forth with charges of cruelty if flagrant examples of abuse or death occur. To document abuses, attend the event and have a video camera and a couple of witnesses besides yourself on hand.
- After the event, once more ask the sponsor to find a replacement event next time. If the negative

publicity has been affective, the sponsor may now well concede.

If you need further assistance in halting these events, contact your regional office of the Humane Society of the United States. (Refer to the list on page 170.)

47

Invest Your Money Ethically

Most of the luxuries and many of the so called comforts of life, are not only not indispensable, but positive hindrances to the elevation of mankind.

—Henry David Thoreau

Invest your savings in companies, funds, or enterprises that do not exploit animals or damage the environment. More and more investment companies now screen corporations according to social and ecological criteria, and are reaping excellent returns for their clients. In fact, some $450 billion (up from $40 billion in 1984) is currently being invested in mutual funds that promote environmental responsibility, animal welfare, social justice, and alternatives to nuclear energy.

For details on these groups, we recommend *Economics as if the Earth Really Mattered: A Catalyst Guide to Socially Conscious Investing*, by Susan Meeker-Lowry, New Society Publishers, and the *Directory of Environmental Investing*, by Business Publishers, Inc. You may also contact Co-op Amer-

ica, 2100 M Street NW, Washington, DC 20036;
(202) 872-5307.

Ethically Responsible Investment Companies

Advest, Inc., 124 Mount Auburn Street, Cambridge, MA 02138; (800)
876-6673; (617) 876-5700 in Massachusetts.

Boettcher and Co., 828 17th Street, Denver, CO 80202; (800) 525-
6482; (303) 628-8314 in Colorado.

Calvert Social Investment Fund, 1700 Pennsylvania Avenue NW,
Washington, DC 20006; (800) 368-2748.

Financial Alternatives, 1514 McGee Avenue, Berkeley, CA 94703; (415)
527-5604.

Interwest Financial Advisers, Inc., P. O. Box 790, Salem, OR 97308;
(503) 581-6020.

PAX World Fund, 224 State Street, Portsmouth, NH 03801; (603) 431-
8022.

Prescott, Ball & Turben, 230 West Monroe, 28th floor, Chicago, IL
60606; (800) 621-6637; (312) 641-7800 in Illinois.

The Social Responsibility Investment Group, Inc., The Candler
Building, Suite 622, 127 Peachtree Street NE, Atlanta, GA 30303;
(404) 577-3635.

Solid Investments, Inc., 101 West Street, Hillsdale, NJ 07642; (201)
358-1212.

United Services Fund, P. O. Box 29467, San Antonio, TX 78229-0467;
(512) 696-1234.

Working Assets Funding Services, 230 California Street, Suite 500,
San Francisco, CA 94111, (415) 989-3200. Largest socially
responsible money-market fund in the United States screens out
companies with a history of environmental violations and does
not invest in nuclear power.

Of course, it is often difficult to rate a corporation
in terms of its concern for animals, especially since
many companies are part of huge corporate con-
glomerates with many diverse, complex parts. But

you need not buy stock only in companies that are perfect. For instance, why not buy stock in McDonald's and then push for a stockholder resolution to serve veggie burgers? Indeed, in 1989, a record number of shareholder resolutions demanded an end to product testing on animals, and other animal-protection steps. Even if these resolutions are not passed, they still raise corporate awareness, forcing companies to examine their practices and get back to shareholders on progress made.

For information on shareholder resolutions, contact Investor Responsibility Research Center, 1755 Massachusetts Avenue NW, Washington, DC 20036; (202) 939-6500.

Change the Law

■

The greatness of a nation and its moral progress can be judged by the way its animals are treated.

—Mahatma Gandhi

During the past few years, a number of states have begun passing animal-protection laws that go way beyond today's anti-cruelty statutes. Existing statutes prohibit blatant animal abuse. The new laws, however, cover a much broader base, dealing with issues from protection of endangered species to humane treatment of unwanted pets. Many animal-rights activists and humanitarians hope to protect animals through federal laws. We have found, however, that state and local laws can be far more effective when it comes to animal rights.

In California alone, for instance, a number of good animal laws are now on the books. Among other things, they:

- Mandate sterilization of cats adopted from public pounds.
- Mandate protection for endangered species.

- Mandate humane care for animals in pet shops.
- Prohibit use of live vertebrate animals in scientific experiments in public elementary and high schools.
- Prohibit the possession of any live cat other than a house cat for all except zoos and scientific institutions.
- Prohibit use of the metal-jawed bear trap.
- Prohibit the use of high-altitude decompression chambers for euthanasia.

Similar laws have been passed in states including Florida, Massachusetts, New Jersey, Rhode Island, Connecticut, Maine, Washington, and Virginia.

To pass a law in your state, county or municipality, follow these steps:

1. Analyze the issue. Clearly grasp the problem you face, and formulate, in your mind and on paper, the best solution. Do you need new legislation, or will your problem be solved if laws already on the books are enforced? Check with your local animal-welfare organization and your local law enforcement agency to see what laws are already on the books, and what their impact has been. To find out about existing state laws, contact the secretary of state or attorney general in your state capital. Also research the history of your issue through local newspapers and magazines.

2. Decide whether to start locally or pursue your issue at the state level. Remember, it is often easier to get a local ordinance passed. We like the slogan "think globally, act locally." Animal-rights and -welfare concerns may be global in scope, but local action is often the most efficient way to help. Once a local law has been passed, you will have extra momentum for bringing your issue before a state body. Once you have chosen your forum, research the legislative body that you will approach: How often does it meet? How many members does it have? Which committee will oversee proposed legislation on your issue? Do you need a sponsor to represent your cause? If so, whom should you ask to help? To find a sponsor sympathetic to your issue, contact your local Humane Society.

3. *Write your legislation.* Make sure that the legislation you write is direct and to the point, covering only one issue. If you want to outlaw trapping, for instance, do not include other changes in hunting laws in your proposed bill. If the bill covers too many issues, it will have to contend with many special-interest groups and committees; chances of passage would be small. For help in writing your legislation you may contact your legislative body or the local bar association. You may also know an attorney who would volunteer his or her services. You may find that another state or area has already enacted the kind of legislation that you are seeking. Get a copy of that bill and use it as a working model for your own. As you write your bill, examine the cost that its passage would incur. If passage of your bill will cost nothing, or eventually save money, point that out.

4. *Make sure you are heard.* Try to get the appropriate committee to schedule hearings on your bill. The most effective means of accomplishing that is showing strong public interest in the topic. Have your friends and neighbors write to their representatives, and to the local newspaper to bolster support. You can even hold press conferences and issue

press releases to advance your cause. Also, make appointments to see representatives on the appropriate committee individually. Assume that these individuals know little about the issue, and provide them with a clear, concise fact sheet. (Avoid lengthy handouts.) Answer any questions that the representative may have. Remember, be honest. Present your point of view, but explain what the opposition is likely to claim, as well. This will add to your credibility. During hearings, make sure that you back up your arguments with as much evidence as possible.

5. *Know your friends and enemies*. Your bill will have a better chance of passing if it has diverse support. Therefore, find other local groups that are interested in your issue and ask them to publicize your cause at their meetings and in their newsletters. For instance, church groups may join you to oppose horse and dog racing in the community because these activities invite gambling, and possibly drug-dealing. By the same token, be aware of your adversaries. Do they employ a lobbyist to influence legislators? Do they spend large sums of money on advertising? Is the material they present accurate, or is it biased? What arguments do they generally use against your issue? You and your friends must know as much as possible about your opponents in order to prepare an effective counter-campaign.

6. *Psyche out the executive branch*. It's always a good idea to know how the government executive, be it the governor or the mayor, feels about your issue. After all, this person has the power to veto your bill even after it has passed in the legislative body. Once you learn how the executive feels, you

can try to gain this person's support before the legislation reaches his or her desk.

Every so often you will want to *fight* legislation that has been introduced by somebody else. To discover bills being introduced, have your name put on the mailing list for your legislative body and other interested groups. Once you have discovered an offensive bill, you will have to campaign against it using many of the same tactics previously described to pass a bill. Make sure your point of view is heard. Meet with legislators. And try to reach—and influence—the executive who has the ultimate authority to veto the bill.

For legal advice in any area of the animal-protection field, write to the Animal Legal Defense Fund, a nationwide network of more than two hundred attorneys, at 1363 Lincoln Avenue, San Rafael, CA 94901.

49

Contact Your Legislators on Important Animal Issues Now Before the House and Senate

■

The purpose of law is to prevent the strong from always having their way.

—Ovid

The legislative process is slow-moving, and the status of a bill can remain the same for months. While the action may seem to stop, however, the bill is often moving through the committee process, where legislators hear all the pros and cons. It is very important that during the drawn-out committee process your legislators hear from you on these issues.

All representatives are addressed: The Honorable ———, House of Representatives, Washington, DC 20515.

All senators are addressed: The Honorable ———, U.S. Senate, Washington, DC 20510.

When you write to legislators, mention the specific bill number and spell out your views. Always thank them for their attention.

If you decide to call instead, the congressional switchboard number is (202) 224-3121. But a letter is more effective than a call.

By the way, bills with the prefix *S., S. Con,* or *S. J. Res* originate in the Senate. Bills with the prefix *H. R., H. Con,* or *H. J. Res* originate in the House of Representatives.

For information on a wide range of federal and state bills, join the Humane Society of the United States so that you can receive its *Animal Activist Alert,* which summarizes all pending federal legislation on animal- and environmental-protection issues. You can also lobby for animal legislation on the grassroots level through the National Alliance for Animal Legislation, P. O. Box 75116, Washington, DC 20013; (703) 684-0654.

50

Become an Official Animal Advocate

■

I am in favor of animal rights as well as human rights. That is the way of a whole human being.

—Abraham Lincoln

Get appointed to your state wildlife commission or to the animal-care-and-use committee at a nearby university. You may also apply for a job as a congressional staffperson dealing with the environment and animals, or work in your school district as a humane educator or environmentalist.

Before seeking an official position, of course, we suggest that you work at the grassroots level in the field of animal or environmental protection. As you gain experience and become involved in such advocacy work, you will receive an education that no university has yet offered.

To prepare yourself for a more official position, we also suggest that you attend training workshops on animal advocacy, often held at annual conferences sponsored by major animal-protection and conservation organizations.

Once you feel that you have a sufficient education, you may opt for an official position yourself. Such positions tend to create themselves when you happen to be in the right place at the right time. Being a volunteer is often the first step to becoming a full-time advocate. For many people this has meant a change of profession and life-style and a new life with more meaning and purpose. Some take courses at college or night school to learn about animal care, wildlife rehabilitation, humane education, animal-facilitated therapy, animal and environmental law, or work as an intern for an advocacy organization.

APPENDIX A

ANIMAL BILL OF RIGHTS

Animals have the right to equal and fair consideration and to be treated with humane concern and responsibility.

Animals have the right to live free from human exploitation, whether in the name of science or sport, exhibition or service, food or fashion.

Animals have the right to live in harmony with their nature, rather than in accordance with human desires.

Animals have the right to live on a healthy planet.

Endangered species have the right to life and habitat preservation.

Animals have the right to be protected from physical or mental suffering when subject to any form of human exploitation for which there is no alternative; and every effort should be made to develop appropriate alternatives.

Domestic animals have the right to live in adequate physical and social environments.

Animals have the right to be regarded as "ours" only in sacred trust.

APPENDIX B

RESOURCE GUIDE

I. HISTORY OF THE HUMANE MOVEMENT AND THE TREATMENT OF ANIMALS

Brown, Anthony. *Who Cares for Animals?: 150 Years of the RSPCA*. London: Heinemann, 1974.

Carson, Gerald. *Men, Beasts, and Gods: A History of Cruelty and Kindness to Animals*. New York: Charles Scribner's Sons, 1972.

Magel, Charles R. *A Bibliography on Animal Rights and Related Matters*. Washington, DC: University Press of America, 1981.

McCrea, Roswell C. *The Humane Movement*. College Park, MD: McGrath Publishing Company, 1969.

Niven, Charles D. *History of the Humane Movement*. New York: Transatlantic Arts, Inc., 1967.

Salt, Henry. *Animals' Rights*. 1892. Reprint. Clark Summit, PA: Society for Animal Rights, 1980.

Thomas, Keith. *Man and the Natural World: A History of Modern Sensibility*. New York: Pantheon, 1983.

Turner, James. *Reckoning with the Beast: Animals, Pain, and Humanity in the Victorian Mind*. Baltimore: The Johns Hopkins University Press, 1980.

II. ETHICAL AND PHILOSOPHICAL ISSUES

Clark, Stephen. *The Nature of the Beast: Are Animals Moral?* New York: Oxford University Press, 1982.

Clark, Stephen R. L. *The Moral Status of Animals*. New York: Oxford University Press, 1977.

Favre, David S., and Loring Murray. *Animal Law*. Westport, CT: Quorum Books, 1983.

Fox, Michael W. *Inhumane Society: The American Way of Exploiting Animals*. New York: St. Martin's Press, 1990.

———. *Animals Have Rights Too*. (A book for children.) New York: Crossroads, 1990.

———. *Returning to Eden: Animal Rights and Human Concerns*. Malabar, Florida: Robert E. Krieger, 1986.

———. *Between Animal and Man*. Malabar, Florida: Robert E. Krieger, 1984.

———. *One Earth, One Mind*. Malabar, Florida: Robert E. Krieger, 1985.

Linzey, Andrew. *Christianity and the Rights of Animals*. New York: Crossroads, 1987.

Midgley, Mary. *Animals and Why They Matter*. Athens, GA: University of Georgia Press, 1984.

Regan, Tom. *The Case for Animal Rights*. Los Angeles: University of California Press, 1983.

Rollin, Bernard E. *Animal Rights and Human Morality*. Buffalo, New York: Prometheus Books, 1981.

Schweitzer, Albert. *The Teaching of Reverence for Life*. New York: Holt, Rinehart & Winston, 1965.

Singer, Peter. *Animal Liberation*. 2nd ed., rev. New York: Random House, 1990.

III. LABORATORY AND FARM ANIMALS

Dawkins, Marian Stamp. *Animal Suffering: The Science of Animal Welfare*. London: Chapman and Hall Ltd., 1980.

Fox, Michael W. *Agricide: The Hidden Crisis That Affects Us All*. New York: Schocken Books, 1986.

———. *Laboratory Animal Husbandry: Ethology, Welfare, and Experimental Variables*. Albany, New York: State University of New York Press, 1986.

———. *Farm Animals: Husbandry, Behavior, and Veterinary Practice*. Baltimore: University Park Press, 1984.

Harrison, Ruth. *Animal Machines*. London: Vincent Stuart Publishers Ltd., 1964.

Lawrence, E. A. *Rodeo: An Anthropologist Looks at the Wild and the Tame*. Nashville: University of Tennessee Press, 1982.

Mason, Jim, and Singer, Peter. *Animal Factories*. New York: Crown Publishers, Inc., 1980.

Pratt, Dallas, M.D. *Alternatives to Painful Experiments on Animals.* New York: Argus Archives, 1982.

Regan, Tom, ed. *Animal Sacrifices: Religious Perspectives on the Use of Animals in Science.* Philadelphia: Temple University Press, 1986.

Robbins, John. *Diet for a New America.* Walpole, NH: Stillpoint, 1987.

Rollin, Bernard. *The Unheeded Cry: Animal Consciousness, Animal Pain, and Science.* New York: Oxford University Press, 1989.

Ryder, Richard D. *Victims of Science: The Use of Animals in Research.* rev. ed. London: National Anti-Vivisection Society, 1983.

Schell, Orville. *Modern Meat.* New York: Random House, 1984.

Sharpe, R. *The Cruel Deception: The Use of Animals in Medical Research.* Wellingborough, England: Thorsons Publishers, Ltd., 1988.

IV. ANIMALS: WILD, CAPTIVE, AND ENVIRONMENTAL CONCERNS

Baker, Ron. *The American Hunting Myth.* New York: Vantage Press, 1985.

Berry, Thomas. *The Dream of the Earth.* San Francisco: Sierra Books, 1988.

Devall, Bill, and Sessions, George. *Deep Ecology: Living as if Nature Mattered.* Salt Lake City: Gibbs M. Smith, Inc., 1985.

Domalain, Jean-Yves. *The Animal Connection: The Confessions of an Ex-Wild Animal Trafficker.* New York: William Morrow, 1977.

Ehrlich, Paul, and Ehrlich, Anne. *Extinction: The Causes and Consequences of the Disappearance of Species.* New York: Random House, 1981.

Hediger, H. *Man and Animal in the Zoo: Zoo Biology.* New York: Delacorte Press, 1969.

Leopold, Aldo. *A Sand County Almanac.* New York: Oxford University Press, 1966.

Nash, R. F. *The Rights of Nature: A History of Environmental Ethics.* Madison, WI: University of Wisconsin Press, 1989.

V. COMPANION ANIMALS

Fox, Michael W. *The Healing Touch*. New York: Newmarket Press, 1990.

———. *Love is a Happy Cat*. New York: Newmarket Press, 1990.

———. *The New Animal Doctor's Answer Book*. New York: Newmarket Press, 1990.

———. *Supercat: Raising the Perfect Feline Companion*. New York: Howell Books, 1990.

———. *Superdog: Raising the Perfect Canine Companion*. New York: Howell Books, 1990.

———. *Behavior of Wolves, Dogs and Related Canids*. Malabar, Florida: Robert E. Krieger, 1984.

———. *The Dog: It's Domestication and Behavior*. Malabar, Florida: Robert E. Krieger, 1985.

Kay, W. J., with Randolph, E. *The Complete Book of Cat Health*. New York: Macmillan Publishers, 1985.

———. *The Complete Book of Dog Health*. New York: Macmillan Publishers, 1985.

Lorenz, Konrad Z. *King Solomon's Ring: New Light on Animal Ways*. New York: Thomas Y. Crowell, 1952.

Pitcairn, R. H., and Pitcairn, S. H. *Natural Health for Dogs and Cats*. Emmaus, PA: Rodale Press, 1982.

Tuan, Yi-Fu. *Dominance and Affection: The Making of Pets*. New Haven: Yale University Press, 1984.

VIDEO AND AUDIO TAPES

Silent World: Genetic Engineering, Biotechnology
45-minute ½-inch VHS video discusses ethical, environmental, agricultural, and animal-welfare concerns associated with this new technology—$20.00 (includes postage). Script only—$1.50.

Steps Toward a Humane Sustainable Agriculture
35-minute ½-inch VHS video reviews the serious problems of modern intensive agriculture and details the economic, environmental, consumer health, and farm-animal-welfare benefits of alternative husbandry practices—$20.00 (includes postage). Script only—$1.50.

Animals, Nature, and Religion
35-minute ½-inch VHS video explores the teachings of the world's major religions as they relate to our perception and treatment of our fellow creatures and the Earth's creation—$18.00 (includes postage). Script only—$1.50.

The State and Future of Creation
20-minute audio cassette. $6.00 (includes postage).

CENTER FOR RESPECT OF LIFE AND ENVIRONMENT
An affiliate of The Humane Society of the United States
2100 L Street, NW
Washington, DC 20037
(202) 452-1100

If you have any additional ideas or thoughts on protecting or saving the animals, please don't hesitate to write to the authors, % Richard Romano, St. Martin's Press, 175 Fifth Avenue, New York, NY 10010.

**The Brilliant Biography
of the Woman who Wrote—
and Lived—
OUT OF AFRICA**

Isak Dinesen
The Life of a Storyteller

JUDITH THURMAN

_____ 90202-6 $4.95 U.S.   _____ 90203-4 $5.95 Can.

WINNER OF THE AMERICAN BOOK AWARD

"Isak Dinesen was everything a biographer could wish for:
an extraordinary writer and an even more extraordinary
woman who behaved as if she were a character in one of her
own Gothic tales....This remarkably good book is rich."
—*The New York Times*